Toast

Also by Nigel Slater

Real Fast Food
30-Minute Cook
Real Cooking
Real Good Food
Nigel Slater's Real Food
Appetite
Thirst

Toast

The story of a boy's hunger

Nigel Slater

FOURTH ESTATE · *London* and *New York*

First published in Great Britain in 2003 by
Fourth Estate
A Division of HarperCollins*Publishers*
77–85 Fulham Palace Road
London W6 8JB
www.4thestate.com

10 9 8 7 6 5 4 3 2 1

A catalogue record for this book is available from the
British Library

ISBN 1-84-115289-7

Typeset by Rowland Phototypesetting Limited,
Bury St Edmunds, Suffolk.
Printed in Great Britain by
Clays Ltd, St Ives plc

For Digger, Magrath and Poppy
with love

In memory of Elvie 1902–2002

I would like to thank Louise Haines, Araminta Whitley and Allan Jenkins for their support, patience and encouragement, and Justine Picardie, who commissioned the short story, first published in the *Observer*, on which this book is based.

Toast 1

My mother is scraping a piece of burned toast out of the kitchen window, a crease of annoyance across her forehead. This is not an occasional occurrence, a once-in-a-while hiccup in a busy mother's day. My mother burns the toast as surely as the sun rises each morning. In fact, I doubt if she has ever made a round of toast in her life that failed to fill the kitchen with plumes of throat-catching smoke. I am nine now and have never seen butter without black bits in it.

It is impossible not to love someone who makes toast for you. People's failings, even major ones such as when they make you wear short trousers to school, fall into insignificance as your teeth break through the rough, toasted crust and sink into the doughy cushion of white bread underneath. Once the warm, salty butter has hit your tongue, you are smitten. Putty in their hands.

Christmas Cake

Mum never was much of a cook. Meals arrived on the table as much by happy accident as by domestic science. She was a chops-and-peas sort of a cook, occasionally going so far as to make a rice pudding, exasperated by the highs and lows of a temperamental cream-and-black Aga and a finicky little son. She found it all a bit of an ordeal, and wished she could have left the cooking, like the washing, ironing and dusting, to Mrs P., her 'woman what does'.

Once a year there were Christmas puddings and cakes to be made. They were made with neither love nor joy. They simply had to be done. 'I suppose I had better DO THE CAKE,' she would sigh. The food mixer – she was not the sort of woman to use her hands – was an ancient, heavy Kenwood that lived in a deep, secret hole in the kitchen work surface. My father had, in a rare moment of do-it-yourselfery, fitted a heavy industrial spring under the mixer so that when you lifted the lid to the cupboard the mixer slowly rose like a corpse from a coffin. All of which was slightly too much for my mother, my father's quaint Heath Robinson craftsmanship taking her by surprise every year, the huge mixer bouncing up like a jack-in-the-box and making her clap her hands to her chest. 'Oh heck!' she would gasp. It was the nearest my mother ever got to swearing.

She never quite got the hang of the mixer. I can picture her now, desperately trying to harness her wayward Kenwood, bits of cake mixture flying out of the bowl like something from an *I Love Lucy* sketch. The cake recipe was written in green biro on a piece of blue Basildon Bond and was kept, crisply folded into four, in the spineless *Aga*

Cookbook that lived for the rest of the year in the bowl of the mixer. The awkward, though ingenious, mixer cupboard was impossible to clean properly, and in among the layers of flour and icing sugar lived tiny black flour weevils. I was the only one who could see them darting around. None of which, I suppose, mattered if you were making Christmas pudding, with its gritty currants and hours of boiling. But this was cake.

Cooks know to butter and line the cake tins before they start the creaming and beating. My mother would remember just before she put the final spoonful of brandy into the cake mixture, then take half an hour to find them. They always turned up in a drawer, rusty and full of fluff. Then there was the annual scrabble to find the brown paper, the scissors, the string. However much she hated making the cake we both loved the sound of the raw cake mixture falling into the tin. 'Shhh, listen to the cake mixture,' she would say, and the two of us would listen to the slow plop of the dollops of fruit and butter and sugar falling into the paper-lined cake tin. The kitchen would be warmer than usual and my mother would have that I've-just-baked-a-cake glow. 'Oh, put the gram on, will you, dear? Put some carols on,' she would say as she put the cake in the top oven of the Aga. Carols or not, it always sank in the middle. The embarrassing hollow, sometimes as deep as your fist, having to be filled in with marzipan.

Forget scented candles and freshly brewed coffee. Every home should smell of baking Christmas cake. That, and warm freshly ironed tea towels hanging on the rail in front of the Aga. It was a pity we had Auntie Fanny living with us. Her incontinence could take the edge off the smell of a chicken curry, let alone a baking cake. No matter how many mince pies were being made, or pine logs burning in the grate, or how many orange-and-clove pomanders my mother had made, there was always the faintest whiff of Auntie Fanny.

Warm sweet fruit, a cake in the oven, woodsmoke, warm ironing, hot retriever curled up by the Aga, mince pies, Mum's 4711. Every child's Christmas memories should smell like that. Mine did. It is a pity that there was always a passing breeze of ammonia.

Cake holds a family together. I really believed it did. My father was a different man when there was cake in the house. Warm. The sort of man I wanted to hug rather than shy away from. If he had a plate of cake in his hand I knew it would be all right to climb up on to his lap. There was something about the way my mother put a cake on the table that made me feel that all was well. Safe. Secure. Unshakeable. Even when she got to the point where she carried her Ventolin inhaler in her left hand all the time. Unshakeable. Even when she and my father used to go for long walks, walking ahead of me and talking in hushed tones and he would come back with tears in his eyes.

When I was eight my mother's annual attempt at icing the family Christmas cake was handed over to me. 'I've had enough of this lark, dear, you're old enough now.' She

4

had started to sit down a lot. I made only marginally less of a mess than she did, but at least I didn't cover the table, the floor, the dog with icing sugar. To be honest, it was a relief to get it out of her hands. I followed the Slater house style of snowy peaks brought up with the flat of a knife and a red ribbon. Even then I wasn't one to rock the boat. The idea behind the wave effect of her icing was simply to hide the fact that her attempt at covering the cake in marzipan resembled nothing more than an unmade bed. Folds and lumps, creases and tears. A few patches stuck on with a bit of apricot jam.

I knew I could have probably have flat-iced a cake to perfection, but to have done so would have hurt her feelings. So waves it was. There was also a chipped Father Christmas, complete with a jagged lump of last year's marzipan round his feet, and the dusty bristle tree with its snowy tips of icing. I drew the line at the fluffy yellow Easter chick.

Baking a cake for your family to share, the stirring of cherries, currants, raisins, peel and brandy, brown sugar, butter, eggs and flour, for me the ultimate symbol of a mother's love for her husband and kids, was reduced to something that 'simply has to be done'. Like cleaning the loo or polishing the shoes. My mother knew nothing of putting glycerine in with the sugar to keep the icing soft, so her rock-hard cake was always the butt of jokes for the entire Christmas. My father once set about it with a hammer and chisel from the shed. So the sad, yellowing cake sat round until about the end of February, the dog giving it the occasional lick as he passed, until it was thrown, much to everyone's relief, on to the lawn for the birds.

Bread-and-Butter Pudding

My mother is buttering bread for England. The vigour with which she slathers soft yellow fat on to thinly sliced white pap is as near as she gets to the pleasure that is cooking for someone you love. Right now she has the bread knife in her hand and nothing can stop her. She always buys unwrapped, unsliced bread, a pale sandwich loaf without much of a crust, and slices it by hand.

My mother's way of slicing and buttering has both an ease and an awkwardness about it. She has softened the butter on the back of the Aga so that it forms a smooth wave as the butter knife is drawn across it. She spreads the butter on to the cut side of the loaf, then picks up the bread knife and takes off the buttered slice. She puts down the bread knife, picks up the butter knife and again butters the freshly cut side of the loaf. She carries on like this till she has used three-quarters of the loaf. The rest she will use in the morning, for toast.

The strange thing is that none of us really eats much bread and butter. It's like some ritual of good house-keeping that my mother has to go through. As if her grandmother's dying words had been 'always make sure they have enough bread and butter on the table'. No one ever sees what she does with all the slices we don't eat.

I mention all the leftover bread and butter to Mrs Butler, a kind, gentle woman whose daughter is in my class at school and whose back garden has a pond with newts and goldfish, crowns of rhubarb and rows of potatoes. A house that smells of apple crumble. I visit her daughter Madeleine at lunchtime and we often walk back to school together. Mrs Butler lets me wait while Madeleine finishes her lunch.

'Well, your mum could make bread-and-butter pudding, apple charlotte, eggy bread, or bread pudding,' suggests Mrs Butler, 'or she could turn them into toasted cheese sandwiches.'

I love bread-and-butter pudding. I love its layers of sweet, quivering custard, juicy raisins, and puffed, golden crust. I love the way it sings quietly in the oven; the way it wobbles on the spoon.

You can't smell a hug. You can't hear a cuddle. But if you could, I reckon it would smell and sound of warm bread-and-butter pudding.

Sherry Trifle

My father wore old, rust-and-chocolate checked shirts and smelled of sweet briar tobacco and potting compost. A warm and twinkly-eyed man, the sort who would let his son snuggle up with him in an armchair and fall asleep in the folds of his shirt. 'You'll have to get off now, my leg's gone to sleep,' he would grumble, and turf me off on to the rug. He would pull silly faces at every opportunity, especially when there was a camera or other children around. Sometimes they would make me giggle, but other times, like when he pulled his monkey face, they scared me so much I used to get butterflies in my stomach.

His clothes were old and soft, which made me want to snuggle up to him even more. He hated wearing new. My father always wore old, heavy brogues and would don a tie even in his greenhouse. He read the *Telegraph* and *Reader's Digest*. A crumpets-and-honey sort of a man with a tight little moustache. God, he had a temper though. Sometimes he would go off, 'crack', like a shotgun. Like when he once caught me going through my mother's handbag, looking for barley sugars, or when my mother made a batch of twelve fairy cakes and I ate six in one go.

My father never went to church, but said his prayers nightly kneeling by his bed, his head resting in his hands. He rarely cursed, apart from calling people 'silly buggers'. I remember he had a series of crushes on singers. First, it was Kathy Kirby, although he once said she was a 'bit ritzy', and then Petula Clark. Sometimes he would buy their records and play them on Sundays after I had listened to my one and only record – a scratched forty-five of Tommy Steele singing 'Little White Bull'. The old man was inordinately fond of his collection of female vocals. You should have seen the tears the day Alma Cogan died.

The greenhouse was my father's sanctuary. I was never sure whether it smelled of him or he smelled of it. In winter, before he went to bed, he would go out and light the old paraffin stove that kept his precious begonias and tomato plants alive. I remember the dark night the stove blew out and the frost got his begonias. He would spend hours down there. I once caught him in the greenhouse with his dick in his hand. He said he was just 'going for a pee. It's good for the plants.' It was different, bigger than it looked in the bath and he seemed to be having a bit of a struggle getting it back into his trousers.

He had a bit of a thing about sherry trifle. That and his dreaded leftover turkey stew were the only two recipes he ever made. The turkey stew, a Boxing Day trauma for everyone concerned, varied from year to year, but the trifle had rules. He used ready-made Swiss rolls. The sort that come so tightly wrapped in cellophane you can never get them out without denting the sponge. They had to be filled with raspberry jam, never apricot because you couldn't see the swirl of jam through the glass bowl the way you could with raspberry. There was much giggling over the sherry bottle. What is it about men and booze? They only cook twice a year but it always involves a bottle of something. Next, a tin of peaches with a little of their syrup. He was meticulous about soaking the sponge roll. First the sherry, then the syrup from the peaches tin. Then the jelly. To purists the idea of jelly in trifle is anathema. But to my father it was essential. If my father's trifle was human it

9

would be a clown. One of those with striped pants and a red nose. He would make bright yellow custard, Bird's from a tin. This he smoothed over the jelly, taking an almost absurd amount of care not to let the custard run between the Swiss roll slices and the glass. A matter of honour no doubt.

Once it was cold, the custard was covered with whipped cream, glacé cherries and whole, blanched almonds. Never silver balls, which he thought common, or chocolate vermicelli, which he thought made it sickly. Just big fat almonds. He never toasted them, even though it would have made them taste better. In later years my stepmother was to suggest a sprinkling of multicoloured hundreds and thousands. She might as well have suggested changing his daily paper to the *Mirror*.

The entire Christmas stood or fell according to the noise the trifle made when the first massive, embossed spoon was lifted out. The resulting noise, a sort of squelch-fart, was like a message from God. A silent trifle was a bad omen. The louder the trifle parped, the better Christmas would be. Strangely, Dad's sister felt the same way about jelly – making it stronger than usual just so it would make a noise that, even at her hundredth birthday tea, would make the old bird giggle.

You wouldn't think a man who smoked sweet, scented tobacco, grew pink begonias and made softly-softly trifle could be scary. His tempers, his rages, his scoldings scared my mother, my brothers, the gardener, even the sweet milkman who occasionally got the order wrong. Once, when I had been caught not brushing my teeth before going to bed, his glare was so full of fire, his face so red and bloated, his hand raised so high that I pissed in my pyjamas, right there on the landing outside my bedroom. For all his soft shirts and cuddles and trifles I was absolutely terrified of him.

The Cookbook

The bookcase doubled as a drinks cabinet. Or perhaps that should be the other way around. Three glass decanters with silver labels hanging around their necks boasted Brandy, Whisky and Port, though I had never known anything in them, not even at Christmas. Dad's whisky came from a bottle, Dimple Haig, that he kept in a hidden cupboard at the back of the bookcase where he also kept his Canada Dry and a jar of maraschino cherries for when we all had snowballs at Christmas. The front of the drinks cabinet housed his entire collection of books.

The family's somewhat diminutive library had leather-ette binding and bore Reader's Digest or The Folio Society on their spines. Most were in mint condition, and invariably 'condensed' or 'abridged'. Six or so of the books were kept in the cupboard at the back, with the Dimple Haig and a bottle of advocaat; a collection of stories by Edgar Allan Poe, a dog-eared Raymond Chandler, a Philip Roth and a neat pile of *National Geographics*. There was also a copy of Marguerite Patten's *All Colour Cookbook*.

It was a tight fit in between the wall and the back of the bookcase. Dad just opened the door and leaned in to get his whisky; it was more difficult for me to get round there, to wriggle into a position where I could squat in secret and turn the pages of the hidden books. I don't know how Marguerite Patten would feel knowing that she was kept in the same cupboard as *Portnoy's Complaint*, or that I would flip excitedly from one to the other. I hope my father never sells them. 'For sale, one copy each of Marguerite Patten's *All Colour Cookery* and Philip Roth's *Portnoy's Complaint*, first edition, d/w, slightly stained.'

'I don't know what you want to look at that for,' said Mum once, coming home early and catching me gazing at a photograph of Gammon Steaks with Pineapple and Cherries. 'It's all very fancy, I can't imagine who cooks like that.' There was duck à l'orange and steak-and-kidney pudding, fish pie, beef Wellington and rock cakes, fruit flan and crème caramel. There was page after page of glorious photographs of stuffed eggs, sole with grapes and a crown roast of lamb with peas and baby carrots around the edge, parsley sprigs, radish roses, cucumber curls. Day after day I would squeeze round and pore over the recipes fantasising over Marguerite's devilled kidneys and Spanish chicken, her prawn cocktail and sausage rolls. Just as I would spend quite a while fantasising over Portnoy's way with liver.

The Lunch Box

Josh, Mum and Dad's new gardener, was cool. He had a black motorbike, a Triumph something or other, and used to bring his lunch neatly packed in a tin box. He licked his cigarette papers, tiny things with barely a pinch of tobacco in them, and rolled them into short flat cigarettes while he sat on his bike. Everyone liked Josh, Mum thought he was 'such a good-looking young man, as bright as a button', and Dad seemed more happy with him than he had been with the older guys who used to leave almost as soon as they had started. One was fired just because the frost got at Dad's dahlias.

Unlike the other gardeners, Josh used to let me turn the compost with the long-handled, two-pronged fork that no one else let me touch and empty the mower box on to the heap. He let me weed the front of the borders where we had planted daisy-faced mesembryanthemums that only came out in the sun and balls of alyssum and drifts of pink and white candytuft. I watched the way he tied the clematis up when the string broke once in the wind, and when he used to pee on the compost. 'Better not tell your dad I do that, it's my secret way of getting the compost to work,' he would say, turning as he shook himself and did up his buttons.

My father smiled, beamed almost, when I called plants by their proper names. *Antirrhinum* instead of snapdragon and *Muscari* instead of grape hyacinth. He gave a tired but amused little snuffle when I once corrected him about the name of a rose that he had called Pleasure when I knew it was Peace. Josh would take me round the borders, getting me to name as many plants as I could and would tease me when I confused azaleas and rhododendrons. Sometimes he would hoist me up on to his bare shoulders and charge around the garden making airplane noises and pretending to crash into the trees. We played football once, but my saves were so bad that the ball, an orange one belonging to my brothers, kept crashing into the marguerites and knocking them flat.

I liked the way Josh would let me sit and talk to him while he took a strip-wash in the outside toilet and changed back into his motorbike leathers. The way he would let me choose a biscuit – a Bourbon, a ginger nut, even a caramel wafer – from his lunch box and the way he never turned his back on me when he was drying himself with his frayed green-and-white-striped towel.

Jam Tarts

A great deal was made of my being tucked in at night. 'I'll come up and tuck you in' was as near as my mother ever got to playing with me. Tucking me in was her substitute for playing ball, going to the park to play on the slide, being there on sports day, playing hide-and-seek, baking cakes, giving me chocolate kisses, ice cream, toffee apples, making masks and carving Halloween pumpkins. 'I'll come up and tuck you in' was fine. It's when she forgot that it wasn't.

Every few weeks my mother and I would make jam tarts. She had small hands with long, delicate fingers. Gentle, like her name, Kathleen, and that of her siblings, Marjorie and Geoffrey. They say there was some Irish blood somewhere, but like my mother's asthma no one ever spoke of it.

She would weigh the flour, the butter, the bit of lard that made the pastry so crumbly, and let me rub them all together with my fingertips in the big cream mixing bowl. She poured in cold water from a glass and I brought the dough together into a ball. Her hands started work with the rolling pin, then, once the ball of pastry was flat, I would take over, pushing the pastry out into a great thin sheet. We took the steel cookie cutters, rusty, dusty, and cut out rings of pastry and pushed them into the shallow hollows of an even rustier patty tin.

Mother didn't like cooking. She did this for me. When she met my father she was working as a secretary to the mayor at the town hall and had never made so much as a sandwich. My father's first marriage had lasted only a matter of months and was never, ever discussed. (By sheer chance, an old acquaintance of my father's asked my brother if he was from the first or second marriage. Otherwise we would never have known.) She fell pregnant with me fifteen years after my brother Adrian was born and five years after they adopted his schoolfriend John. That's when the asthma came on. When she was expecting me.

There had to be three different jams in the tarts. Strawberry, blackcurrant and lemon curd. It wasn't till later I learned that plum, damson and marmalade made the best fillings. I put a couple of spoonfuls of jam into each pastry case, not so much that they would boil over and stick to the tin, but enough that there was more jam than pastry. My father loved a jam tart and would put one in whole and swallow it like a snake devouring a bird's egg. Despite training as a gunsmith, he now owned a factory where they made parts for Rover cars, a factory that smelled of oil, where the machines were black and stood in pools of oily water. 'A man was killed in that one there – he got his overall caught in the roller and it pulled him straight through, flat as a pancake,' my father told me one day as we walked through the black hangar at dusk, its iron roof dripping and the stench of rust around us.

The tarts went in the top oven of the Aga until the edges of the pastry cases turned the pale beige of a Lincoln biscuit and the jam had caramelised around the edges. As the kitchen became hotter and more airless my mother would take her inhaler from the top drawer and take long deep puffs, turning her face away as she did so. Sometimes, she would hold her hand to her chest and close her eyes for a few seconds. A few seconds in which the world seem to stop.

My mother was polite, quietly spoken, but not timid. I

once heard her telling off the delivery boy from Percy Salt's the grocer because there was something on the bill that shouldn't have been. I never heard her raise her voice. I am not sure she could have done if she wanted to. She certainly never did to me.

One day my father came home from work, and even before he had taken off his coat he grabbed one of our jam tarts from the wire cooling rack. He couldn't have known they had come from the oven only a minute or two before. His hands flapped, his face turned a deep raspberry red, beads of sweat formed like warts on his brow, he danced a merry dance. As he tried to swallow and his eyes filled with the sort of tears a man can only summon when he has boiling lemon curd stuck to the roof of his mouth, I am sure that I saw the faintest of smiles flicker across my mother's face.

Spaghetti Bolognese

'We ... are ... going to have ... spaghetti, no, SPAG-HETTI ... just try a bit of it. You don't have to eat it if you DON'T LIKE it.' Mum is yelling into Auntie Fanny's 'good' ear. Quite why she thinks there is a good one and a bad one is a mystery. Everyone knows the old bat is deaf as a post in both.

Neither Fanny nor Mum has eaten spaghetti before, and come to think of it neither have I. Dad is waiting for the water to boil on the Aga. The sauce is already warm, having been poured from its tin a good half-hour ago and is sitting on the cool plate of the Aga, giving just the occasional blip-blop.

When the water finally boils my father shakes the strands of pasta out of the blue sugar paper that looks for all the world like a great long firework, and stands them in the bubbling water. They splay out like one of those fibre-optic lights we saw at the Ideal Home Exhibition on the BBC. As the water comes back to the boil he tries to push the spikes under the water. 'They'll never all go in,' he snaps, trying to read the packet, which, even when read with bifocals, is in Italian. Some of the brittle sticks break in half and clatter over the hotplate.

'Will I like it, Daddy?' I ask, half hoping he'll change his mind and Mum will cook us all some chops.

'Just try it,' he says, a somewhat exasperated tone creeping in to his voice. 'Just try it.'

'I think you should put some salt in,' chirps in Mum.

Auntie Fanny is looking down at her lap. 'Do I have to have some?' I think she is going to cry.

'I think it must be done now,' says my father twenty minutes later. He drains the slithery lengths of spaghetti in a colander in the sink. Some are escaping through the holes and curling up in the sink like nests of worms. 'Quick, get the plates, they're getting away.'

We all sit there staring at our tumbling piles of pasta on our glass Pyrex plates. 'Oh, Kathleen, I don't think I can,' sobs Auntie Fanny, who then picks up a long sticky strand with her fingers and pops it into her mouth from which it hangs all the way down to her lap.

'No, wait for the sauce, Fanny,' Mother sighs, and then quite out of character, 'Come on, Daddy, hurry up.' Dad spoons the sauce, a slurry of reddy-brown mince that smells 'foreign', over the knots and twirls of pasta. Suddenly it all seems so grown-up, so sophisticated.

Mum wraps the strands round her fork, 'like this, do it like this,' then shovels it towards Fanny's wet, pink little lips. Most of the pasta falls down Fanny's skirt, a little of the sauce gets caught on her bottom lip. She licks it off and shudders. 'It's horrible, it's horrible. He's trying to poison me,' she wails. We all know she would have said the same even if it had been the most delectable thing she had ever eaten.

Ignoring Fanny's little tantrum, I do as Mother bids, twirling the pasta round my fork while shovelling the escaping pieces back on with my spoon. I rather like it, the feel of the softly slippery noodles, the rich sauce which is hot, salty and tastes partly of tomato, partly of Bovril. I wouldn't mind eating this every day. Unexpectedly, my father takes out a cardboard drum of grated Parmesan cheese and passes it to me to open.

'What's that you've got there?' asks Mum.

'It's grated cheese, Percy Salt said you have to sprinkle it over the top, it doesn't work if you don't.' Now we're talking. I peel away the piece of paper that is covering the holes and shake the white powder over my sauce. I pass it to my father who does the same. Mum declines as she usually does with anything unusual. There is no point in asking Auntie Fanny, who is by now quietly wetting her pants.

Dad shakes the last of the cheese over his pasta and suddenly everyone goes quiet. I'm looking down but I can see my father out of the corner of my right eye; he has stopped, his fork in mid-air, a short strand of spaghetti hanging loose. His eyes have gone glassy and he puts his fork back down on his plate.

'Daddy, this cheese smells like sick,' I tell him.

'I know it does, son, don't eat it. I think it must be off.'

We never had spaghetti bolognese or Parmesan cheese again. Or for that matter, ever even talked about it.

Arctic Roll

There were only three of us at school whose house wasn't joined to the one next door. Number 67 Sandringham Road, always referred to as 'York House', had mock-Tudor wooden beams, a double garage of which one half doubled as a garden shed and repository for my brothers' canoes, and a large and crumbling greenhouse. I was also the only one ever to have tasted Arctic Roll. While my friends made do with the pink, white and brown stripes of a Neapolitan ice-cream brick, my father would bring out this newfangled frozen gourmet dessert. Arctic Roll was a sponge-covered tube of vanilla ice cream, its USP being the wrapping of wet sponge and ring of red jam so thin it could have been drawn on with an architect's pen.

In Wolverhampton, Arctic Roll was considered to be something of a status symbol. It contained mysteries too. Why, for instance, does the ice cream not melt when the sponge defrosts? How is it possible to spread the jam that thin? How come it was made from sponge cake, jam and ice cream yet managed to taste of cold cardboard? And most importantly, how come cold cardboard tasted so good?

As treats go, this was the big one, bigger even than a Cadbury's MiniRoll. This wasn't a holiday or celebration treat like trifle. This was a treat for no obvious occasion. Its appearance had nothing to do with being good, having done well in a school test, having been kind or thoughtful. It was just a treat, served with as much pomp as if it were a roasted swan at a Tudor banquet. I think it was a subtle reminder to the assembled family and friends of how well my father's business was doing. Whatever, there was no food that received such an ovation in our house. Quite an achievement for something I always thought tasted like a frozen carpet.

Pancakes

Mum never failed to make pancakes on Shrove Tuesday. Light they were, except for the very first one which was always a mess, though for some reason always the best. Mum made thin pancakes, in a battered old frying pan that was black on the outside and smelled of sausages, and we ate them with granulated sugar and Jif lemon. I loved the way the lemon soaked the sugar but never quite dissolved it, so you got the soft pancake, gritty sugar and sharp lemon all at once.

It was the best day of the year really, especially when she got going and they would come out of the pan as fast as we could eat them. Towards the end Mum would let me flip one. I always contrived it so that it landed on the floor, then she would say, 'That's enough', and that would be it till next year.

Flapjack

On crackling winter mornings, with icicles hanging from the drainpipes, Mother would make flapjacks, stirring them in a thick, pitted aluminium pan and leaving them to settle on the back of the Aga. She would use a metal spoon, which acted as an effective alarm clock as it was scraped against the side of the old pan. They were one of the very few treats my mother ever made for us. My father would eat one or two, probably to encourage her rare attempts at home-making. While I would have to be held back from eating the entire tray. It was their chewy, salty sweetness I loved. Anyone who has never put a really large pinch of salt in with the oats, syrup and brown sugar is missing a trick.

Sometimes, she would leave a flapjack out for Josh too, and we would sit on his motorbike and eat them together. One bitterly cold day, I came home to a hall that smelled of warm biscuits. As I opened the kitchen door I smelled smoke and caught my mother tossing a batch of blackened flapjacks into the bin. There was a bit of charred shrapnel clinging to the edge of the tin which I tried unsuccessfully to prise off. Now they were being tipped into the pedal bin, tray and all. 'I'm sorry, darling,' she said, shaking her head. There were tears and something along the lines of 'How could you do that, let the flapjacks burn? You're hopeless, now there won't be any for Josh tomorrow,' and then I remember stomping into the greenhouse and telling my father he should get a new wife. One who didn't burn everything.

Percy Salt

If you walked along Penn Road past the fish shop and towards the stately pile that is the Royal School for Boys, you came to Percy Salt's the grocer's. It was two shops really, a butcher's on the right and on the left a cool, tiled grocer's that had sawdust on the floor and where my mother did most of her shopping. It was here she bought the ham that the young assistants in long white aprons would cut to order from the bone; slices of white-freckled tongue for Dad and tins of peaches and thick Nestlé's cream for us all. This was where we came for streaky bacon, for sardines and, at weekends, for cartons of double cream.

Percy Salt's was the only place where my mother ran a tab. It was the custom for the better-off clientele, as was having their purchases delivered. This was where I would stand while Mum asked to taste the Cheddar or the Caerphilly and where she would pick up round boxes of Dairylea cheeses for me. Sometimes there would be little foil-wrapped triangles of processed cheese flavoured with tomato, celery (my favourite), mushroom and blue cheese. This was also where we came for butter and kippers, salad cream and honey, eggs and tea.

I loved our visits to Salt's like nothing else. It was the smell of the shop as much as anything, a smell of smoked bacon and truckles of Cheddar, of tomatoes in summer and ham hocks in winter. At Christmas the windows would light up with clementines in coloured foil, biscuits in tins with stagecoaches on the lids, fresh pineapples, whole peaches in tins, trifle sponges and packets of silver balls and sugared almonds. Mother would buy wooden caskets of Turkish delight and crystallised figs, sugared plums and jars of cherries in brandy. It was here too that she would collect the brandy for the brandy butter, the bottles of Mateus Rosé, the cartons of icing sugar and the chocolate Christmas decorations that we hung on the tree and that I would sneak one by one over the holidays. Never was I happier than in Percy Salt's at Christmas, even if my mother did once say he was getting 'terribly dear'.

'Dear', when used in connection with money, was one of the expressions for which my mother would lower her voice, just as she did when she found someone 'rather coarse' or when someone had 'trodden in something'. 'Have you trodden in something' was my mother's discreet way of asking if you had farted. No surprise then that while Mr Salt called most of his customers 'love' he would always, always call my mother Mrs Slater.

Sweets, Ices, Rock and Politics

It would be wrong to say we were wealthy. 'Comfortably off' might be nearer the mark, though without the implied smugness. There were tinned peaches and salmon on the shopping list but Mum still checked Percy Salt's delivery scrupulously, running her finger down the list and ticking things off with a blue biro. Dad took cuttings and planted seeds – yellow snapdragons, nemesia the colour of boiled sweets, and those daisy-faced mesembryanthemums that only opened up when the sun shone – because it was cheaper than buying ready-grown bedding plants. Needless to say I had no more pocket money than any of my school friends.

I bought the odd book, annuals mostly, a few singles, 'Can't Buy Me Love' or Dusty Springfield's 'I Only Want

To Be With You', and once, a stick insect, but most of my pocket money went on sweets. Buying sweets, chocolate, even ice cream was shot through with more politics than an eight-year-old should have had to contend with. Sweets could put a label round a child's neck in much the same way as a particular choice of newspaper could to an adult. For a boy certain things were off-limits. Fry's Chocolate Creams and Old English Spangles were considered adult territory; Love Hearts and Fab ice creams were for girls. Parma Violets were for old ladies and barley sugars were what your parents bought you for long car journeys. Cones filled with marshmallow and coated in chocolate were considered naff by pretty much everyone, though I secretly liked them, and no one over six would be seen dead with a flying saucer. Sherbet Fountains were supposed to be strictly girly material, an idea which even then I refused to buy into. Milky Ways were what parents bought for their kids, which gave them a sort of goody-goody note as did Jacob's Orange Clubs. Selection boxes were what you were given at Christmas by the sort of people who weren't relatives but who nevertheless you called Auntie.

We never really bought the penny chews that Mr Dixon had loose on the counter, though I did nick the odd liquor-ice chew, the ones that came in blue-and-white striped paper, when his back was turned. Dad's favourites were Callard & Bowser's Butterscotch, which came in thin packs like cigarettes, and Pascall's oblong Fruit Bonbons with gooey centres. He also loved peanut brittle, which he ate by the barful. Mine were sweet cigarettes, which may not have given me lung cancer but made up for it with fillings. At Christmas, Dad bought himself metal trays of Brazil nut toffee with their own little hammer from Thorntons, while I got more cigarettes, this time made of chocolate wrapped in paper which went soggy when you put it in your mouth. Dad said they were expensive. Mum only ate sweeties that came in round tins, old-fashioned things like lemon drops and fruit pastilles with a faint dusting of icing sugar or those chewy blackcurrant gums that came in a flat white-and-purple rectangular tin.

Boys' stuff, by which I mean gobstoppers, Milky Bars and Rolos, never really hit the spot for me. I spent most of my money on sweets that made your tongue sore: acid drops, sherbet lemons, chocolate limes and roll after roll of Refreshers. The price for which was mouth ulcers the size of shirt buttons, and on which I would put salt-and-vinegar crisps to see just how much pain I could stand.

Holidays meant sticks of rock, pink or humbug-striped with red letters running through it. I never ate mine till I had kept it for at least six months in the fruit bowl. By which time it had gone soft and chewy, like mint-flavoured toffee.

Your choice of ice cream depended more on who was buying. Mum would get me a cornet with a rectangle of vanilla ice cream wrapped in white paper. It was an ice fraught with danger. You had to peel off the paper and push the block of ice cream down into the cornet while at the same time licking every last, precious drop of vanilla from the paper. For herself, she would get a little block of ice cream wrapped in paper and two wafers, or a choc ice in foil. The best bit was the crackly chocolate which was so thin that it would shatter and fall off into her lap in jagged pieces. At the cinema or the pantomime we always had tubs, though my father invariably complained about the price and having to queue for so long that the second half had started before he got back to his seat.

My parents disapproved of the ice-cream van, with its pineapple Mivvis and belching smoke. I found the music – wobbly, like a music box running down – faintly sinister, like those clowns with white faces and pointed hats. I think my parents just thought it was common to queue. My favourite was the banana lolly or the chocolate one which tasted like weak cocoa. Mum drew the line at Mr Whippy cornets, which she considered beyond the pale, and 99s were simply vulgar. Heaven knows what she would have said if she had seen me on my way to school, biting off the end and sucking the soft, grainy ice cream through the bottom.

Rice Pudding

Mother was desperate to be a homemaker, a woman capable of sewing on a button, darning a sock or icing a fairy cake. In the early evening, sitting under the standard lamp in the lounge, head tilted and the tip of her tongue pinched between her lips, she spent what seemed like hours trying to thread white cotton through the eye of a needle. 'Let me do it' was met with a sigh and 'I've nearly done it now'. Try as she might, buttons popped off within a day or two, toes poked through neat but ineffective repairs, icing pooled into the craters in her cakes or, on the rare occasion they rose, ran down the sides in rivulets and stuck the flowery paper cases to the plate.

Mrs Poole made the beds, fed the winceyette sheets through the ironing machine with its long cotton-covered roller, and would sew a stray button on to my school shirt. Mother made up for this humiliation by making rice pudding. Warm, milky rice. Rice that never thickened the sweet liquid it floated in, so what should have been a creamy spoonful the texture of risotto had to be sipped, like broth. The skin browned and puffed into a black-and-gilt dome. The kitchen smelled like a kitchen should.

The skin was removed in one perfect scoop and deposited in my father's bowl. 'It's the best bit,' he used say. Then the round rice was fished up from the depths and divided between us all. Then she would pick up the enamel tin and spoon out the milk. 'Anyone for jam?' she would say, passing round the Hartley's strawberry. I was the only taker, stirring the sweet glop into the milk then regretting it when it stayed in blobs and sank to the bottom of the dish.

Milky milky rice is considered a failure by rice-pudding

aficionados, yet I preferred it to her occasional successes. Warm sweet milk was what a mother should smell of.

Butterscotch Flavour Angel Delight

BUTTERSCOTCH FLAVOUR: Sugar, Modified Starch, Hydrogenated Vegetable Oil, Emulsifiers (Propane-1, 2-diol esters of fatty acids, Soya Lecithin), Gelling Agents (Disodium phosphate, Diphosphates), Milk Protein, Lactose, Colours (Plain Caramel, Annatto, Betanin), Whey Powder, Flavourings, Salt.

Emptying a sachet of Angel Delight into half a pint of milk and whisking it for a minute and a half was as near as my mother ever got to making modern desserts. She remembered which flavour – Strawberry, Butterscotch, Chocolate or Banana – she had served last, and never risked boring us with the same flavour twice in a row. Butterscotch and Banana were the only truly acceptable flavours to us. We ate the others to humour her.

Butterscotch Angel Delight was magic. Magic in the way that if you stood over it for five minutes you could actually watch the powder and milk thicken into a creamy dessert. Magic in the way it seemed to thicken further once you put it in your mouth. Magic in what seemed like a mean portion in the bowl became almost too much of a good thing in the mouth. Magic in the way that it managed to taste of both sugar and soap at the same time.

Mashed Potato

At least twice a week my mother would make mashed potato and pile it in great, buttery, cloud-like mounds next to boiled gammon or lamb chops. It was the one thing my mother couldn't get wrong. But then, good mash isn't about cooking. It's about the ability to beat lumps out of a cooked potato. Anyone could do that. Except, apparently, a school dinner lady. Mash was the only truly glorious thing Mum ever made.

There was no moment so perfect as when you squished her mashed potato into warm parsley sauce or hot gravy with your fork. The soft potato pushing up in wavy lines through the gaps between the prongs, curling over on itself, stained with dark drops of gravy. No roast potato stuck to its roasting tin; no crinkle-cut chip; no new potato with chopped mint could ever get the better of a dollop of creamy mash. I looked forward to it like I looked forward to nothing else.

One day I came home from school to find my mother sitting there at the kitchen table, her head bent down towards her lap, her eyes closed, her chest heaving slowly and deeply. She had started to do this rather a lot recently. It was as if there was something that she had to concentrate on, something she could only do by closing out the rest of her senses.

Today the potatoes were grainy and salty, wet but possessed of a dry, almost powdery feel in the mouth. 'The mash tastes funny, Mummy.' Quietly and firmly, in a tone heavy with total and utter exasperation, and with a distant rasp after the first word, she said, 'Nigel ... Just eat it.'

As soon as she went upstairs, I climbed down from the table to scrape the offending spud into the bin. Tucked under the packet that once held the frozen peas was a maroon-and-black packet I had never seen before. In large creamy-white letters were the words Cadbury's Smash.

Tinned Ham

It's a Saturday in mid-August and we have dragged the picnic table on to the lawn. My mother likes it to sit between the apple trees so she doesn't have to squint in the sunshine. She is wearing Scholl sandals and a duck-egg blue dress with sprigs of daisies. It has buttons up the front. She and my father bring the food out from the kitchen while I just sit at the table looking at my lap. There's a bowl of pale lettuce, some slices of beetroot in vinegar, cucumber cut so thin you could read the Bible through it and a sauce boat of Heinz Salad Cream. We must be the only family in Britain to put salad cream in a sauce boat.

My mother puts a tomato on my plate and cuts it in quarters, then a few giant curls of lettuce, two slices of beetroot and tells me, 'You don't have to have salad cream if you don't want to.' I know what's coming. My father is eyeing my plate, searching for the slice of ham that will turn his puny son into a Viking warrior.

Without a word he stabs his fork into a slice of ham and slaps it on my plate. A hot wave of hate goes through my body. Hate ham, hate him.

Actually, I rather like ham. What I don't like is this ham. The sort of ham that comes from an oval green tin and is surrounded by golden-brown jelly. The sort of ham it takes an age to prise from its aluminium coffin. The sort of ham that my father carves very thinly with the same knife he uses for the Sunday roast. Pretty-pink ham, evil jelly.

It is amazing how long it can take to scrape every morsel of jelly from a slice of cold boiled meat. I spend a good fifteen minutes separating good from bad, pushing the jelly towards the edge of my plate. A scientist exhuming a mummified corpse wouldn't have been as patient as I am. Meanwhile, my father is glaring at me with a mixture of anger and disgust. Disgust at what I am not quite sure. Could it be the waste of valuable protein or the waste of valuable time? Could it be simply that it looks ungrateful? Perhaps it is the way I am doing it, like someone has put poo on my plate.

Mother is silent, Father is silently fuming. If he were a cartoon you'd see the smoke coming out of his ears.

Suddenly, he reaches across the table, picks up my plate with its ham, salad and painstakingly removed jelly and chucks it across the lawn. Mother pulls her lips into a thin, straight line. Ham, beetroot, lettuce and cucumber are spread out on the lawn. I get down from table and run in through the kitchen and upstairs to my bedroom. I close the door, lie face down on the bed and wait.

Space Dust

If you opened a sachet of the original Space Dust and poured it into your mouth, the little citrus and chemical beads crackled and hissed like you had put your tongue on a battery. If you poured three packets in at once, it was like putting your tongue on an electric fence. This is probably why they changed the formula.

Auntie Fanny looks so bored sitting in her chair, the one with the rubber liner for when she wets her long winceyette pants. The ones that come down to her knees. You feel you want to brighten her day. Sometimes I sit and talk to her even though I know she can't hear a word I am saying. I can say rude words to her like willy and bum and she just smiles at me and hums. Sometimes we swap sweets. She gets my chocolate buttons, I get her Parma Violets. I once gave her a Toffo but it stuck her dentures together. Mum said that sometimes I can be a little thoughtless.

She looks so bored sitting there, humming to herself. I'm sure Auntie Fanny would enjoy a sachet of Space Dust. Maybe even two. Or even three.

'Mum . . . Mum . . . Auntie Fanny's doing it AGAIN.'

Bombay Duck

Not only has my brother got *A Hard Day's Night*, a pair of desert boots and a donkey jacket with leather patches on the elbows, he's even been to an Indian restaurant. It is easy to hate someone like that. He thinks it's time I experienced the scented delights of chicken biryani and lamb vindaloo and takes me, together with our other brother John, to the Kohinoor, a small flock-wallpapered Indian restaurant tucked behind the rollerdrome in Wolverhampton.

The restaurant is almost empty and smells of armpits. 'I'm going to have a Bombay duck and a chicken biryani,' says Adrian as soon as we're seated. John goes for the chicken vindaloo, then they start laughing about something called the Ring of Fire, which doesn't seem to be on my menu. It must one of the 'specials'. The menu is terrifying, though not half so much as the man in a turban standing at the kitchen doorway, his arms folded in front of him. It is like he is daring us to set foot in the kitchen.

'I can't manage both, I'll just have the Bombay duck,' I say timidly. It sounds exotic, even more so than chicken

Madras. Adrian asks me if I know what Bombay duck is and I assure him I do. He and John seem to find something funny. Adrian then orders a biryani for me too, despite my pleading, and insists I will manage both.

We get a pile of giant crisps as big as a plate and some spicy gunk to dip them in that makes my nose run and my ears sting. They order beers and I drink my first ever shandy. My brothers say it's only like drinking pop, but even so not to mention it to Dad. The Bombay duck arrives – a wizened bit of grey bark smelling like something that has been dead a very long time. Putrid. 'It's not like I had it last time,' I say rather grandly, without thinking the fib through thoroughly.

The lone waiter in evening dress brings the biryanis and John's vindaloo. I am not at all sure about this. The room smells of mildew and beer and the aforementioned arm-pits and the man on the kitchen door hasn't smiled once since we arrived. The waiter smells funny too and his suit is shiny round the collar. The chicken is dark and strongly flavoured, browner than I have ever known chicken to be. Adrian tells me not to play with my food and just eat it. 'Are you sure this chicken's all right?' I ask, poking at the hedgehog-coloured meat like it was poisoned.

'Yes, it's the spices that make it that colour,' assures John, who seems to know quite a bit about Indian food.

I gingerly swallow a few mouthfuls. Actually, I probably could eat more but there is something I don't like about this place. Something sinister, something a little 'grubby'. Adrian suddenly snaps, 'You little sod, you've hardly eaten anything.'

A couple of weeks later I gleefully cut a piece out of the *Express and Star* (usually pronounced in its catchment area as the Expressenstar) and leave it on the kitchen table. It is story about health inspectors finding skinned cats hanging up in the fridges of Indian restaurants.

Blackcurrant Pie

Mother is upstairs, having forty winks, as she calls her afternoon nap. Adrian is standing in the doorway, smiling and swaying back and forth. His eyes flicker open and closed. He stumbles over to the sofa with its white cotton covers with their sprigs of flowers, stands at the end of it then falls backwards on to the sunken cushions. He lies there on his back, his eyes open then close, then he crosses his hands on his chest like Boris Karloff and goes to sleep.

Adrian got Hush Puppies this week, slip-ons the colour of a roe deer. The ones with the black elastic patches at the side. They look great with his narrow black knitted tie and his white button-down shirt. Mum has promised to take me shopping to Beau Brummell's for a button-down shirt for school. She says I can't have a tie like his because I will never wear it and suede shoes will last all of five minutes with me. She reckons I grazed my new sandals, horrid red-brown ones with diamonds cut into the toes within two days. She says she doesn't believe me when I tell her that Maxwell Mallin and Peter Francis jumped on them in the playground at lunchtime. Then, after a pause to get her breath, she snaps, 'It wouldn't happen if you'd play with the other boys.' It is one of our rare icy moments. It occurs to me that if she died I would be allowed to wear a black tie to school.

Josh has come to do the garden but sees my brother asleep and says he has to go back home and will come again on Monday. I follow him out to the drive but he seems distant, cold even. I explain that my brother is a really nice guy but Josh doesn't want to know, he just revs up and drives off. Distant. 'I'll see you then.'

When I come back Adrian is in a different position, and the sofa seems to have mysteriously moved forward a good two feet. The rooms smells of tinned chicken soup and something sour.

There is the sound of a key in the door and my father pops his head round the door. 'Adrian's asleep, Mum's asleep,' I say, even though it probably doesn't need saying. Daddy stares intently at my brother, screwing up his eyes like he is trying to work something out. 'Hmm,' he grunts.

On the kitchen table is a large, cardboard box with short sides. A large sandwich loaf, a packet of butter, two bags of white sugar, a bunch of red, blue, white and magenta anemones, a blackcurrant pie, a box of Terry's All Gold and the *Radio* and *TV Times*. My father brings more stuff up out of the boot of the Rover and puts it down on the table, grabs the box of All Gold and takes it back to the car and puts it in the glovebox. He then hands me a box of Mackintosh's Weekend and tells me to take it upstairs to Mum.

By the time I'm back down – she's asleep – he's cut each of us a slice of blackcurrant pie, sliding the thin slices on to glass Pyrex plates. This is the pie I think about all week. The pie I lie in bed and dream about before I go to sleep. The fruit is sharp and sweet, the pastry pale and crumbly, like it is only just about cooked. It has no decoration save a small hole like a navel in the middle. Sometimes it isn't quite in the centre. I don't understand this, why would you put it off-centre? I eat my pie slowly, pushing my fork down through the sugar crust and into the purple-blue fruit below.

Someone thumps the huge knocker on the door twice. I can hear Warrel, my best friend. 'Can Nige come out to play?' My father pokes his head around the door. 'Well, can he?' 'Nigel can't come out just now, he isn't feeling well,' I say, biting my lip. My father smiles and disappears. Play with my best friend or have second portions of pie? No contest.

I take my second slice of pie into the sitting room. Adrian has disappeared upstairs. I sit on the floor, my back resting against the sofa. It slides back on its castors to its original position. There, where the edge the sofa had been, is a pile of my brother's warm vomit. But pie is pie and I tuck in regardless.

Grilled Grapefruit

There was a brief time when I was the coolest kid at school. My brother had bought *Rubber Soul* and I listened to it, lights low, when he was out for the evening with his girlfriend who had long blonde hair and eyes so heavy with mascara she looked like a panda. I learned every word by heart. Only about two kids at school had even heard of it, and I knew every single word. Not even my brother, who knew everything, knew all the words. He thought 'Michelle' was crap. I thought it was brilliant. Little did I know my brother was far too busy shagging old panda eyes in the back of his Hillman Imp to learn the words to *Rubber Soul*.

It was about this time my father bought a grapefruit knife. It was heavily serrated with a blade that curved like a children's slide. Just think, we were so sophisticated, so glamorous, so cool we actually had a special knife to cut our grapefruits. I didn't know anyone else who even had grapefruits.

The first time we ate grilled grapefruit was something of a performance. We had all heard about them, though none of us knew anyone who had actually had one, so we had to guess how they were done. My father shook a thick layer of granulated sugar over the halved fruit, of course they were all yellow in those days, and got the grill hot.

Getting the grill hot was a bit like 'getting the car out', that peculiar ritual of revving the car up in the garage about half an hour before we went anywhere. 'No, I'll finish packing, you get the car out,' my mother would say. Nowadays, they would take less trouble over starting up a space shuttle. The grill hot, or at least as hot as it ever got, we all stood and watched the sugar melting, most of which slid off the top, down the sides and started to burn in the bottom of the grill pan.

In the panic to find the oven gloves, my father tried to pull the grapefruits out with his bare hands, his eyes watering from the molten sugar. He had even bought special grapefruit spoons with serrated edges. We pulled the loose segments out of their shells, crunching through the half-melted, half-granular sugar. It was very hot and very cold, very sweet and very sour all at once. 'Is this how they're supposed to be,' said someone, not entirely kindly, and we all went rather quiet. But I just thought how utterly cool I was to have eaten grilled grapefruit. I boasted about it to everyone at school the next day in much the same way as someone might boast about getting their first shag.

Cheese and Pineapple

We rarely had visitors who stayed to eat. We had never even been to, let alone given, a dinner party, despite having a dining table that could seat twelve. But there were friends who would appear now and again, usually couples so similar as to be indistinguishable from one another. They had names like Ray or Eunice. All the men wore ties and cardigans. The women wore twinsets. The sort of women who talked about their 'dailies' and would never leave the house without a brooch. I do remember them all laughing a lot, but I never understood what about. Everyone was taller than me. It was as if I wasn't there.

It was my job to pass around the room with the food. Oh God, the food. 'Now, dear, you make certain that everyone gets a cheese football, won't you?' my mother would say. Our place in local society seemed not to depend on whether we had a double garage (we had) or which golf club my father belonged to (he didn't). It was more a question of whether you had Huntley & Palmer's Cheese Footballs or not.

The pièce de résistance was a grapefruit spiked with cocktail sticks holding cubes of cheese and pineapple. The preparation was always a bit of a performance: draining the syrup from the tinned pineapple, cutting the Cracker Barrel into even-sized chunks, finding the cocktail sticks that would usually end up at the back of the gadget drawer covered in a dusting of flour. I hated doing it.

Few things could embarrass a would-be chef quite as much as having to hold out a whole grapefruit speared with cubes of Cheddar and tinned pineapple on cocktail sticks to men in cardigans.

The worst of it was that everyone thought I had done the food. 'He wants to be a chef,' my father would say, as I held up the spiked grapefruit to the Masonic Worshipful Master's wife, who had a tight perm and lips like a cat's bottom. When it came to offering the dreaded grapefruit to everyone else, I would throw my head in the air and flay my nostrils in disapproval. 'Don't pull a face like that,' my father once snapped, 'you look like Kenneth Williams.' But I had to let everyone know my disdain for my parents' catering arrangements. After all, if I had done the food, they would have had prunes wrapped in bacon.

Apples

I played in the garden mostly, away from the road and the big boys with their plastic footballs that stung my legs. 'I'd rather you played where I can see you,' warned Mother, so that suited me fine. Long borders ran either side of the lawn, white rhododendrons, pink- and saffron-coloured azaleas, purple Michaelmas daisies and, in deepest summer, dahlias, spiky ones as big as a dinner plate, maroon and white and gaudy yellow. In one corner was an apple tree, not ours, but most of it overhung our garden, so that come late August its fruit fell into the mauve and white phloxes below.

If I stood on tiptoe I could just reach the apples hanging on the lower twigs, flat-topped apples, pale green and rose like Turkish delight, with snow-white flesh that had ripples of pink running through it. They tasted of strawberries but smelled of the scented phlox that grew underneath them. I could reach these apples, unlike the fruit of the three trees in our garden whose branches were, even on tiptoes, just out of reach. I could get to the glue bands my father put round their trunks though, and used to peel off the flies and wasps they trapped, pulling them by their wings until their bodies came apart.

Uncle Reg used to come round once a week, on a Thursday evening, bringing with him a white paper bag of Cadbury's Flakes, Aztecs, Milky Ways, tubes of Rolo, Munchies, Mintolas and Refreshers and thin black-and-white bars of Caramac. A tall handsome man with sunken cheeks, a slightly hooked nose and shaking hands, the whites of his eyes shot with red veins. He wore a long, grey mackintosh and smelled of something that was both sour and sweet.

Over the summer Uncle Reg came less and less often, his bags of sweets getting bigger with each visit. Sometimes he would bring flowers for my mother. Then one day he stopped coming altogether. I heard my mother on the phone telling someone that he had died. I never saw the lovely Uncle Reg or his sweets again.

There was no limit to how many of next door's apples I was allowed to eat. So I just kept eating them throughout the summer. The largest always fell first, right down through the pink-eyed flowers on their tall stems. At first, I would stretch down into the flowers to pick up the apples until one day I got stung by a wasp hiding in the half-eaten side underneath. Another time there was a maggot jerking its way through the flesh, which I might have missed and eaten if it hadn't been for its tiny dot of a black head. From then on I went in foot first, turning each fruit over with my toe, inspecting for anything that might sting or wriggle.

Cream Soda

Nobody tells me anything. They talk in whispers over my head; in hushed tones when I'm sitting drawing my usual pictures of Scottish hills or gluing model planes together. (I'm very good at shading heather and frankly draw nothing else, inspired no doubt by our last holiday, when we drove back from Loch Lomond with a sprig of the stuff tucked in the radiator of the car.)

Friday afternoon is when the pop man comes. During the summer holidays I wait around for him to arrive so that I can get at the dandelion and burdock before my brothers do. The bottles are heavily embossed and have screw caps that are almost impossible to undo. Favourite: D & B; second favourite: cream soda; least fave is plain lemonade which I leave for everyone else. I think my dad drinks it.

I like dandelion and burdock because it makes me burp really loudly, but the best flavour is actually cream soda. I don't know how they get something clear and pale green to taste creamy but they do.

'I don't know how you can drink that stuff,' says our daily, Mrs Poole, grimacing like a haddock eating mustard. Mrs Poole has long grey hair tied in a plait round her head. Bits of hair, dry and floaty, splay out at all angles so that her plait looks like a viper in a nest. She is fat with a big bottom, actually a vast, flat bottom that sways as she hoovers the sitting room and seems to have a life of its own. You always knew when Mrs P. had been, the house smelled of lavender polish and stale Hoover bags and there was the faintest whiff of armpits. I don't know what my mother would do without her, even though she does smell of tinned tomato soup.

'That stuff'll give you wind,' huffs Mrs P.

'Actually, everything gives me wind.'

'Like you needed to tell me that. I hear you aburpin' an' ablowin' all the time. If your father was to hear those noises you make he'd ban you from drinking all that pop. Sometimes, I'm surprised you don't go bang.'

'Well, if I do, then you'll just have to mop me up, won't you.'

Cream soda never seems as cold as the other drinks. The bubbles are softer, and don't get up your nose and make your sinuses burn like dandelion and burdock or orange-ade. Cream soda looks as if it is going to taste of lime but is instead rather more fleeting, vanilla perhaps. Whatever flavourings they use it is rather like drinking a sponge cake.

Setlers

The most forbidden of places was my father's bedside drawer. I had never been told not to go there; I just knew it was out of bounds. A secret place. An ivory-coloured drawer set in a glossy black table, gold handle, its perfect patina interupted only by a ring burned in the top by a hot mug. My mother's, on the other hand, was an open book. A jumble of tissues and hairpins, powder compacts and violet cachous. Home to one of the many Ventolin inhalers tucked discreetly around the house.

His drawer was neat, and smelled of the cortisone cream he smoothed into his hands in the autumn when each year a weird rash would flare up. There were several opened tubes of Setlers, a little blue Masonic book with dashes where some of the words should be and a fat grey-and-maroon packet of Durex. There were several menus from dinners he had been to, often with the signatures of those who attended on the inside and some strange badges that I guessed were something to do with his Masonic uniform.

Setlers were as much a part of my father's DNA as his pipe and his *Daily Telegraph*. The chalky white tablets went everywhere with him; half and quarter packets were in every jacket pocket, including the one in his suede waistcoat, and in the glovebox of the car. Ten times a day he would rub his sternum and tear another strip of wrapper off his indigestion pills. He would nibble them when he drove and when he watched television. I have even known him take one after supper, 'just in case'. Setlers were my dad's worry beads.

If indigestion presented itself as a side effect of worry, it might also be taken as a symptom for coldness, short temper, impatience and deceit. He suffered all of these, as did we.

The filthiest of Dad's stomach medicines was kaolin and morphine. A thick and creamy white crust that floated on a thin transparent liquid, he called it K et Morph. He would shake the glass bottle for a good two minutes, holding the cork in place with his thumb before he tweaked it out and took a swig, sometimes two, from the bottle. He shuddered as he swallowed during what had become a daily ritual. He always had something disgusting in his mouth, a Setler, a glug of kaolin and morphine, his pipe. When it wasn't one of those it would be Senior Service or a Mannekin. I flinched on the rare occasion he kissed me, even though I wanted him to.

Sunday Roast

The kitchen at York House is in its usual Sunday chaos. Through the clank of pans, I can hear the crackle and spit of roast beef coming from the Aga. My father is in the greenhouse, doing whatever it is that middle-aged men in greenhouses do. Through the hatch I can see steam, which means Mother is draining the beans. Beads of condensation cover the leaded windows. The odd trickle forms pools on the window ledge.

York House is a solid, half-timbered family house, built for new money, with its warren of utility room, scullery, greenhouse and downstairs lavatory. Fashion has it that multicoloured venetian blinds now hang at the leaded-light windows. The garden is somewhat typical of the time; its neat lawn broken by three apple trees with daffodils at the base of their trunks. A majestic willow hangs over the pond and there is a long and winding path around the back. There are bluebells along there, and here and there clouds of London pride.

Roasts are done in the Aga in the main kitchen, vegetables (beans, peas, carrots) on the cream Belling in the scullery. The output from the hottest of the Aga's two hotplates often disappears at the crucial moment. Sunday lunch is almost guaranteed to bring out a sudden drop in temperature. My father says it has something to do with the hot-water supply.

Right now the scullery is hot enough to melt lead.

Though to be fair most of the heat is being given off by my mother, who finds Sunday lunch a meal too many. Her hatred of it is pure and unhidden. She starts to twitch about it on Saturday afternoon. The beef, the potatoes, the beans, the carrots, the gravy, oh God the gravy. Horseradish sauce may or may not appear. It is my father who looks after the twiddly bits, the mustard, 'horserubbish' and the Yorkshire pudding – which he makes in an old roasting tin, one huge pudding, which he cuts into podgy squares. He doesn't do the gravy, but I suspect we all wish he would.

He has a thing about carving the roast. It is like he imagines he clubbed the animal to death and dragged it home through the snow like a caveman with a mammoth. Not to carve the Sunday joint would be an admission to not being quite a man.

How this equates with his love of salmon-pink begonias is another matter.

Heinz Sponge Pudding

Part of the inevitability of Sunday lunch was Heinz Sponge Pudding. I savoured every last crumb, be it raspberry jam, ginger, sultana or chocolate. The last two were what I hoped for when I found the kitchen fugged up with steam and the sound of the tin rattling in its saucepan. The label would fall off and float in the water. I got to learn which one we were having by the smell. Sweet cardboard tinged with chocolate, dried fruit or ginger. To my nose the jam one just smelled of sweet cardboard. There were days when my mother let the pan boil dry and the beloved sultana sponge would burn in its tin. My father would feign nonchalance. It hid his exasperation at having married a woman who couldn't boil water.

A Heinz Sponge Pudding serves four. Just. If we were six for lunch we got two puddings, which meant seconds. If there were five of us my mother would say, 'Oh, one'll do, I won't have any.' But she always would.

We always had cream with our sponge pudding. Nestlé's from a tin, which allowed us to avoid the heartache of watching Mother try to make custard. The cream, so thick you could stand a spoon up in it, was always scooped out of its shallow, white-and-blue tin into the gravy boat and passed round the table. There was a fight, albeit a silent one, to get to the cream jug before Auntie Fanny. Brought up in a family that had never known cream, she was making up for it now, taking almost half the jugful. You could barely see her slice of pudding under it. 'Are you sure you've got enough cream there, Auntie?' my brother would say, followed by a glaring scowl from my father. He aimed it at Adrian but it was just as much meant for Auntie Fanny.

It was essential to get the cream before Fanny for another reason. She had a hooked beak of a nose. An Edith Sitwell sort of a nose. And on the end of that beak there was a permanent dewdrop of thin, clear snot. I can never remember her without it, apart from a few seconds after she wiped it with her flowery hanky and tucked it up the sleeve of one of her baby-blue or lemon cardigans.

When she got to the cream first, five pairs of eyes would focus intently on the glistening bud at the end of her nose, everyone willing the shining bead not to drop until she passed the cream jug on to someone else. Except me. I prayed that one day it would happen, and wondered what everyone would do if it did. Would we have to open another tin? Would my father cover Auntie's embarrassment by just stirring it in and slopping it over his pud? I sat there, my fists clenched in my lap, willing, begging it to happen. I would have relished it. Even more so if no one but me had noticed.

Crisps, Ketchup and a Few Other Unmentionables

I am not certain everything is going well at Dad's factory. He's been quiet lately, pensive, distant, coming in tired and late. I heard him use a low, angry voice on the phone the other night. Another night he looked crestfallen when I went into the kitchen to say hello to him. Like I was a nuisance. He hasn't let me sit on his lap for weeks. 'Not just now,' he says.

He spends a lot of time in deep discussion with my mother and when he laughs it is like he cannot stop, then ends up with tears rolling down his cheeks. After that his mood changes and he lets me climb up on his lap.

My father and his partner Joe Ward built that business up from nothing, taking over a vast disused munitions factory and turning it into something of a gold mine. He employed about twenty men in the factory, a secretary and a clerk who did 'the books'. There used to be an air of excitement, a barely hidden pride about how well the business was doing. He seemed to come home weary now, like he had had enough. Two years earlier, he had been investigated by the Inland Revenue for selling scrap metal from the factory, offcuts mostly, for cash. After that there was more bookwork, so much so that he and my mother used to sit for hours in the kitchen, the table barely visible under piles of receipts on wooden spikes and long hardback books with endless columns of figures and swirly, Florentine endpapers. The two of them could be there all evening, my mother on one side of the table, him on the other. Sometimes he would come and take the whisky bottle and two glasses from the bookcase-cum-drinks cabinet.

I remember one night – they had just started doing 'the books' at home – when I saw something on television about President Kennedy being shot. I went in to the kitchen to tell them he was dead and they told me not to make up stories. 'But it's true, it's on the television,' I pleaded. My father threatened me with a good hiding if I didn't stop telling tales.

'I'm sorry, darling,' Mum said when she came into the sitting room and saw the news unfolding on the television. She just stood there, her hand clasped to her mouth, gasping, 'I just can't believe it.'

'I *told* you,' I said, hot and frustrated that they hadn't believed me.

Half an hour later my father came in with a packet of crisps. 'Have these,' he said. It would be the nearest I would get to an apology. Crisps were frowned upon, rather like baked beans, chips and Love Hearts. Occasionally, he would bring some back from the shops, and I'd open up the crackly bag, poke my fingers right down into the crisps and pull out the bright blue twist of waxed paper that held the salt. Unfurled and shaken into the bag, it was important to get as little of the salt as possible on the crisps. That way, when I had scrunched all the crisps I would have the bonus of finding a thick line of salt at the bottom of the bag to dab up with a wet finger. The salt and the few little crisp crumbs among it were a treat beyond measure, better even than the crisps themselves. This sort of eating wasn't banned, it was simply disapproved of. That was enough. Crisps – light, salty, golden – were banished for the same reason that baked beans were, and fish and chips in newspaper, mushy peas, evaporated milk and sliced bread in plastic. It wasn't that such things were considered bad for me, too sweet or full of additives. It wasn't even because they didn't stock such things at the local grocer. It was because my parents considered them to be 'a bit common'.

The same way they thought petunias and French marigolds were common. The way they thought flip-flops or girls who didn't tie their hair back were common. The same way they considered eating the top layer off a Bourbon biscuit and licking the chocolate filling off was common. Quite how they explained away their predilection for tinned mandarin oranges and Kraft cheese slices is a matter for speculation.

The flip side of their snobbery was that we mostly got to eat good ham, sliced from the bone at Percy Salt's on Penn Road, and to drink Maxwell House coffee. We bought bread from a proper baker's, albeit a white sandwich loaf which my mother found easier to slice that the cute cottage loaves with their wayward topnot. Fish came from the fish shop rather than in breadcrumbed sticks (I didn't taste a fish finger till I was nineteen) and we bought Cadbury's chocolate MiniRolls rather than a plain Swiss roll. We had Battenberg too, and fresh cream and sponges on Saturdays and sometimes waxed cartons of trifle.

Some things were quite unmentionable, even in hushed tones. Babycham, sandwich spread, tomato ketchup, bubble-gum, HP Sauce and Branston Pickle could never even be discussed let alone eaten. Those chocolate marshmallows with biscuit and jam in the middle that came in red-and-silver foil (and which I could cheerfully have killed for) would never have been allowed past the front porch.

Senior Service

Uncle Geoff is wearing his usual tweed jacket, the one that has leather patches on the elbows and smells of Senior Service. He has a tight little moustache, a bit like Adolf Hitler's, shiny yellow teeth and long, thick fingers.

My mother and father are out. Uncle is babysitting. He is on the sofa in the sitting room; I'm snuggled up next to him, breathing in his warm smell of tobacco and wool.

'Do you want to play a game?' he asks. 'It's called Find the Sixpence.'

I close my eyes while Uncle Geoff hides a silver coin. First, I look under the sofa, which we call the settee, then lift each cushion one by one. 'Cold.' I lift the yellow-and-black china plant pot, then the Royal Worcester ashtray and the porcelain black girl with her basket of washing. 'Cold.' On the window ledge is an old lady with a green dress, a string of balloons in her hand. 'Is it under here, Uncle? I'm not supposed to touch her.'

I lift the glass vase with its lone hyacinth, the leather folder that holds the *Radio* and *TV Times*. Cold. 'Is it somewhere on you, Uncle?' 'Getting warmer.' Uncle has tight little pockets on the front of his jacket which will just take a small hand. Cold. I check under his collar and run my fingers down his chequered woollen tie. Uncle Geoff always wears a tie.

Turn-ups, empty. The folds of his maroon V-neck

sweater, empty. The waistband of his trousers, his shoes, empty. I run my hand along the bit of the cushion he's sitting on. 'Getting warmer again.' Uncle's pockets are gaping wide enough for a hand to slip down but then they tighten around the top of his thighs. I push my hand right down into the depths of his pocket, feeling the line of his thigh. I move my hand round over the top of his leg and wriggle it down the inside where his thighs meet. I can feel the edge of a coin but I can't quite get at it. The side of my hand is brushing against something long and hard like the handle of a cricket bat. I slide my hand down its length. It is fatter and softer at one end. Suddenly, as my fingers reach the tip, I can feel the sixpence. Uncle is smiling. 'Warmer, warmer, hot, hot, hot, hot . . .'

Jelly 1

For an eight-year-old boy there is only one true requisite of jelly. And that is that it makes a squelching sound when you dig the spoon deep into its orange depths. A sort of jelly fart. The louder the squelch the better the jelly. Raspberry, orange, lime or strawberry it matters not. The only important thing is the noise. The only way to guarantee the obscenity is to make the jelly stronger than usual. This means using twice as many cubes of jelly. Two packets of jelly cubes to one measure of boiling water. Made this way you get a jelly that farts. It doesn't seem to matter that you then have to eat something that you could play football with.

Jelly 2

I was rarely ill, despite looking as if a good gust of wind would blow me away. There were the usual schoolkid illnesses of course; measles ('stop scratching, you'll only make it worse'), mumps ('better to get it now than later on') and chickenpox ('don't pick them, they'll leave a scar'), but there were few colds and even fewer bouts of flu. There were, however, quite regular occurrences of what my mother christened 'bilious attacks'. These mysterious, short-term fits consisted of faintness, shivering and extreme nausea. I also went as white as milk and distinctly clammy. My father would barely acknowledge their existence. I suspect he felt they were more the sort of thing a bustled Edwardian lady might suffer when her corset was too tight, but they were real enough.

These attacks invariably coincided with maths tests, football practice and the first day of term. I cannot honestly say I faked them – even the best amateur dramatist cannot make someone's skin turn grey, sticky and cold – but it was true that they had a habit of getting me out of things I didn't want to do. Inevitably, the decision would be made to send me to bed for the day.

Being sick meant four things: hot Ribena, tinned soup,

Marmite soldiers and jelly. It was worth a batch of measles to be brought a bowl of Rowntree's blackcurrant jelly on a tray every mealtime. Sometimes Mum would make lime or lemon instead. She used to make it so weak that it only just set, which meant I could suck it through my teeth, the really wibbly wobbly ones slipping off the spoon and down the front of my pyjamas. Jelly was my panacea. It even got me back from one of the worst cases of mumps the doctor said he had ever seen. My father said I looked like Frankenstein's monster.

I cannot say I didn't enjoy being poorly. The sick bucket with its thin layer of evil-smelling disinfectant was never far from my bed, but it was a small price to pay for all the attention, the fact that I didn't have to go to school and the licence to sit in bed all day reading books. Being sick allowed me to reread the 'Narnia' books, *Swallows and Amazons* and all my Malcolm Savilles. The small inconvenience of having a thermometer shoved under my tongue every hour was nothing compared to the joy of snuggling under the yellow candlewick and floating into the land of Narnia.

The worst bit of being ill was being expected to eat tinned soup. Any sensible parent would have boiled up a bowl of jolly-red cream of tomato. The colour alone would have made a poorly boy feel better. Mine tried to woo me back to health with something that bore an uncanny resemblance to what was coming out of either end of me at the time: cream of chicken, cream of vegetable or, in a spectacularly thoughtless moment, oxtail.

Lemon Drops

My mother's mother ended up in Shifnal. A neat, pale blue ward in a hospital that took people whose relatives could no longer cope. There was nothing sinister about it – I remember it being rather pretty, with a rose garden dotted with watery-blue delphiniums the colour of my grand-mother's eyes, and elderly women sitting peacefully in wheelchairs, wearing soft pink- or baby blue-coloured cardi-gans. My mother used to drive me there to see her once a week. Grandmother would sit there smiling, her wispy white hair so thin you could see the freckles on her head, smiling and nodding at everything we said. Even at eight years old I knew she was away with the fairies and would not last long.

Grandmother kept a round tin of lemon drops at her bedside. The sort with a tight lid with pictures of fruit on it. I longed for those sweets. I wanted her to open the tin and offer me one of her golden bon-bons. I wanted to dither over which square sweetie to choose. I dreamed of licking the thin layer of fine icing sugar from them and running my tongue over the little ridges on each side. I longed to dab a wet finger at the loose icing sugar in the bottom and would stare for hours at the golden tin, trying to avoid the plastic beaker next to it. The one with her teeth in.

Our trips to Shifnal, to sit for an hour or two talking to this woman who just smiled and nodded, became more frequent. My mother would pick me up after school two or three times a week, so that while all my classmates played football, I sat in a hospital ward holding the frail, knobbly hands of an old woman who kept her teeth in a mug.

Towards the end, my mother would disappear for ages talking to the ward sister. I knew Grandmother was dying. She would just sit there, smiling and nodding, humming to herself and staring out at the daffodils, pretending not to see the little boy prising the lid off a dying woman's lemon drops.

Milk

My first glass of milk, in truth just two mouthfuls, had ended with my being violently sick over my new sandals. There had been odd attempts to encourage me to try it again, but none had succeeded in getting me to do more than dip my finger in it and shudder. If it looked as if I might be pushed further, a mock heave usually brought the matter to a close. At break times Miss Poole, our mild-mannered, grey-skinned, grey-clothed form teacher allowed any unopened bottles of the compulsory school milk to go to the first to finish.

One cold, flat morning in September I moved up a class. My teacher was now to be Mrs Walker, a woman so stern-faced, so unwaveringly strict as to be used as a threat by the other teachers. She was a stout bulldog of a woman, her unwashed hair pressed tight to her head, dressed as always in a knee-length black skirt and grey twinset. As I picked up my pencil case, my set of twenty Caran d'Ache crayons in their flat tin, my English books with their spelling tests and essays entitled 'An Autumn Day' and 'My Ten Favourite Things', to move up to Mrs Walker's class, someone whispered, 'She makes everyone drink their milk.'

One week later milk had yet to pass my lips. I started offering my small bottle of milk to any girl who would show me her knickers. After getting ripped off a couple of times by girls who failed to keep their part of the bargain, I worried I might have to start paying people to drink my unwanted white stuff.

'Can I have your milk if you don't want it?' asked Peter Marshall one morning break. So I said, 'Show me your dick first,' and with that set a precedent for the whole term. None of the girls wanted an extra bottle enough to give me a quick flash, but the other boys were queuing up for it and perfectly happy with the deal. I think this was the first time I realised food could be a bargaining tool.

Nothing prepared me for how ill a bottle of milk could make a boy. Mrs Walker caught me pretending to drink my ration while waiting for someone to finish theirs. 'Come and stand at the front.' I put my milk on the desk and walked towards her. 'No, bring your milk with you. I've been watching you for days and now you are going to drink it in front of everyone.' Uncertain of just how much of the milk game she had seen, I half wondered whether she was going to make the girls show their knickers to the entire class.

I stood in front of the class, head bent down, my stomach flipping and diving. I worried not about the shame of being caught, but simply that I was going to have to swallow the wretched, wretched milk. Please God, don't let me have to drink this stuff. He didn't answer. 'Drink it all,' said Mrs Walker, her eyes narrowing like a lizard's in bright sunlight. I put the straw to my lips and sucked, sticking my tongue over the open end. 'We will sit here all day until you have finished every drop.'

It was a warm day, mid-September. The milk had been standing in its crate in the sun for a good hour before she sent Robin Matthews to drag it into the classroom. The tinkle of the bottles and scrape of the metal crate always filled me with fear. I sucked. A great bubble of warm, creamy milk hit my tongue, then filled my mouth. It was like vomiting backwards. I tried to swallow slowly, but my throat closed tight and then something acid, almondy, welled up from my stomach.

The vomit came so quickly I didn't have time to move the milk bottle. The straw shot out across the floor, the bottle fell with a clatter and I closed my eyes. Partly to block out the horror of it all and partly because I always close my eyes when I throw up. The puke spluttered down my green school pullover and on to the floor, it splashed the bottom half of the bookcase with its Conan Doyles and Kiplings, Sylvia Mountsey's satchel and a marrow on the harvest festival display. At least it missed my bare legs. When I opened my eyes there was milk over the floor, running under the radiator and Mrs Walker's desk. There was thin, milky-yellow vomit over my shoes and the bottle, whole and unbroken, had rolled under Peter Marshall's desk. 'Go and sit down,' she yelled, ignoring the fact that one of her pupils had just been violently ill down himself. She evidently intended to leave me to stew.

I skulked towards my chair, surrounded by a sea of shy smirks and dropped heads. I bent down to pick up the stray bottle. I got down on all fours and crouched under the table. As I stretched to reach the bottle, something moving caught my eye. It was a flash of three pairs of green knickers and Peter Marshall's dick, fully erect and waving back and forth like a child's flag at a royal walkabout.

PS Nesquik was my parents' last-ditch attempt to make me drink milk. Orange, strawberry, chocolate. The only thing that changed was the colour of my puke.

Peas

'Don't ever, ever go beyond the compost heap,' warned Mrs Saunders, who had a house at the top of the road. We did, of course. Not every time, only when she went out. 'Come on, there's peas.' We went down the rows, picking and popping till we had had our fill. We hid the pea pods in our pockets. When they were full, we tucked the spent pods under the plants, hoping that Mrs Saunders wouldn't see them.

We flicked the peas up in the air, catching them in our gaping mouths. Missing a pea was pathetic. Worse than missing a catch at cricket. We ate just enough. Not to fill our bellies – you cannot fill a child's tummy with peas – just enough that we wouldn't get noticed.

The peas at home were dried Surprise peas, which came in white rectangular boxes so thin and light you might think they were empty. My mother took to Surprise peas like she had been waiting for them all her life. After twenty minutes in boiling water, a Surprise pea was still only the shadow of a pea. Just like my mother's cooking was always a shadow of what it was meant to be. You had just the outside skin. Like someone had stolen the inside. My father said that was the surprise.

To my mother, instant dried peas and carrots were everything she had ever hoped vegetables could be. Quick and effortless to cook and light to carry home. According to Mrs Saunders they were 'ridiculously expensive'. I didn't understand my mother's obsession with things being light to carry home from the shops, that didn't weight her shopping bag down.

Mrs Saunders, of course, grew her own. She planted them in late winter, she would save sticks to support them, cosset them with home-made compost and protect them from the birds with netting and fat strips of green and silver tinsel on sticks. She picked them herself and podded them, a colander in her lap, then boiled them with sprigs of tender mint from her garden and topped with a fat knob of softly melting butter.

My mother emptied a cellophane sachet of dried peas into a pan of water. There was never any mint or butter. Sometimes she even forgot to put salt in the water.

Ice Cream

'Oh I do like to be beside the seaside, Oh I do like to be beside the sea,' sings my father, somewhat predictably, as we come over the brow of the hill, salt air suddenly gusting through the sunshine roof of the car, seagulls squawking on cue. There before us, just as it was last year and the year before (and the one before that), stretches the long beach with its neat frame of formal flower beds. We pass the tall stucco houses that lead down towards the 'front', all sugared almond colours and nodding hydrangeas. 'No vacancies' they proclaim with barely concealed smugness.

My mother starts fussing about a parking place. 'There's one, there, there! Oh, now we've missed it,' she flaps. I point out to my father that we have just missed three on the other side of the road, but I am talking to a man who drives a Rover wearing string-and-leather driving gloves. A man who is no more likely to do a dodgy U-turn than to walk stark naked through the resort's fastidiously preened Winter Gardens.

At last we wiggle our way into a parking space a hundred yards from the hotel. Its paint is peeling more than ever this year. We unpack the unshakeable paraphernalia of the Slater holiday: the striped windbreak, the inflatable beach ball, the picnic basket we have never yet used, my bucket and spade and assorted flags to poke in the top of my intricate sandcastles. Savlon. Bite-eeze. Plasters. Cotton wool. Dettol – the smell of which can make me fall into a dead faint. Mum's spare Ventolin. Some anti-diarrhoea pills. The beach towels that will allow the discreet removal of bathing costumes. The only stuff we buy new each year are bottles of Ambre Solaire – which my dad insists on calling Amber Solaire – and the pastel-coloured plastic windmills that whirl round in the wind and with which I am obsessed.

We have the same rooms as last year. As spotlessly clean as ever, but this year there is an unspoken sadness that hangs over the corridors as surely as if there was a dead seagull strung up over the threshold. We later learn that this is to be the proprietors' final year. They have been getting a different sort of clientele lately – the sort who order morning coffee instead of tea and who don't make their own beds – and have decided to give up. My father talks in hushed tones of moving up to one of the hotels just off the front. Noisier, but you get half-board there and they have a bit of entertainment in the evenings. I wince at the thought of watching my parents dance to the strains of the Ray Miller Combo.

Mother insists on me wearing plastic sandals into the sea. All the other boys on the beach have bare, nut-brown feet. I have red sandals made of plastic so hard they rub blisters into my heels and on the knuckles of my toes. Then my father tries his annual attempt to interest me in ball games. I have to catch the wretched beach ball at the same time as trying to dislodge the sand that has crept inside my sandals and is sticking to the pink skin under my freshly burst blisters. The ball always hits me in the face or brings a shower of sand with it. My father sighs one of those almost imperceptible sighs that only fragile boys who regularly disappoint their father can hear.

We always take lunch at one of the open-air cafés along the beach, Mother desperate for the shade of a parasol. I can see deep-fried fish and chips, with battered plaice the size of a beach tray being brought to the tables by waitresses in tight, pastel dresses and white aprons. We have ham salad. 'Could we have some bread and butter please?' asks Mother, though none of us really wants any.

The meal cannot move on quick enough. I sit there, urging everyone to eat up so that we can get to the ice cream. Why would anyone take their time over a ham salad when there is ice cream to follow? The rules are vanilla, strawberry or chocolate. But even the most acid-tongued old bag of a waitress will let a sweet, blond-haired boy order a ball of each. There's the wafer, of course, a thick, smooth fan if we're lucky, two thin rectangular waffle-wafers if not. I eat them not because they taste good – they are about as flavoursome as a postcard – but because of the way they stick to your bottom lip. My mother likes the wafers more than the ice cream, which to me is a mystery quite beyond comprehension.

There is a moment, shortly after the waitress puts the battered silver coupe of ice cream down on the table, when life is pretty much perfect. I am not sure it is possible to be happier than I am at this moment. I eat all three flavours separately, trying not to let them merge on the spoon. The vanilla and chocolate are OK together, but the strawberry and chocolate don't marry well. As the cold, milky balls of ice cream disappear I scrape up every last drop, the edge of the spoon tinkling on the dented silver dish. I try not to scrape too loudly. Catching Daddy's attention always results in a 'don't be silly' from him. When every last pool of melted ice has gone I use my finger to catch the drips of vanilla ice and the pearls of condensation that have run down the outside of the dish. The cold ice cream in the hot sun is too much for my mother and she turns discreetly away to use her inhaler.

In the evening we walk along the front. I am not allowed on the beach in my best sandals, so we amble slowly along the path, admiring the floral displays. 'How do they do it, it must take them for ever?' marvels Mum, stopping to wonder at a clock made from lobelia and baby begonias. My father is rather taken with a copy of the royal warrant faithfully copied in white alyssum and purple petunias, the words *Dieu et mon droit* picked out in African marigolds. There is, much to everyone's incredulity, not a weed in sight. You could hear the admiring crowd's collective intake of breath as a wayward toddler broke his reins and headed across the grass towards the Queen Mother, so tastefully reproduced in coral-coloured miniature roses and lilac candytuft. His mother got to him in the nick of time. Of course, had he got there first it would have been the highpoint of everyone's holiday, no doubt talked about for years to come.

Enough excitement for one evening. We turn round and walk back, my mother pulling her cardigan over her shoulders as a breeze comes in off the sea. A young guy with wet hair is getting changed by the water fountain. He drops his trunks and pulls on his jeans. 'Excuse ME!' says my father as we all cop a flash of full-frontal nudity.

'Golly,' says my mother, reaching quietly for her inhaler. 'And in Bournemouth.'

Cold Lamb and Gravy Skin

My collection of toy cars filled an entire wooden toy box, the three shelves above my bed and my bedroom window sill. That didn't include the Morris Minor I deliberately crashed into the garden pond or those vehicles sporty enough to be permanently on the mini Monte Carlo rally that spread throughout the entire house. Dinky Chevrolets and Corgi MGs lined up bumper to bumper along every skirting board. Occasionally, one was turned over, the scene of a devastating crash. However, the cars weren't allowed on the stairs. 'Someone will slip and hurt themselves.' This was my licence to send the least valued ones careering headlong down the banisters instead.

My collection was pretty cool. I had the much envied pink Chevrolet Impala, the Corgi Mini Countryman in mint green (the ones where both back doors opened) and even a metallic purple Buick. What I didn't have was the Royal Rolls-Royce. With its glass roof and waving queen, its plastic flag on the radiator and hand-painted royals, it was out of the realm of pocket money. I just had to have it. Nothing would be a bigger sock in the eye for my best friend Warrel Blubb.

Nagging, if done regularly enough and with spirited reasoning rather than a spoiled whine, was a tactic that worked with my parents ... eventually. It could take weeks, sometimes months, but at some point they would come up with the goods. Usually just after I had lost interest and gone on to the next thing. My mother agreed that she would get the Roller for me and let me pay her back at sixpence a week. I knew she would never really ask for the money, doing that thing that parents do of forgetting on purpose. One Saturday morning we walked Wolverhampton for it, but were told over and over again it was out of stock. Then, in a part of town my mother had never dared to set foot in, we found a shop whose owner, a quiet man with owl eyes and wire-framed glasses, who it turned out knew my uncle Geoff, would order one for us. 'Anything for such a sweet boy,' he said.

Rarely was I forced to eat everything on my plate. With my mother's cooking it could have been classed as child abuse. My finicky ways were tolerated as if I was an only child. But occasionally I went over the limit. One cold Monday I had left more of my lunch than usual. It was more a case of boredom than bad cooking. I got down from the table and thought nothing more about it.

That afternoon I got home to find no one in. Sitting in the middle of the dining-room table was my Royal Rolls-Royce, complete with sunroof and lifelike corgis. I picked it up and turned it over and over in my hand. I stroked the long maroon bonnet. Yes, I was disappointed it wasn't the jet black it looked in the photographs but it didn't matter that much. I could barely wait to show Warrel Blubb.

I was hungry to break the news of the car's arrival. I wanted to run round with it then and there. But I could have more fun than that. He had had a telling-off recently – for walking in the house with his wet shoes on. Last time I saw him he was sulking, gazing out of his bedroom window. Vulnerable. I decided to leave the car on the dining-room window sill. That way, he couldn't miss it when he passed on his way to school. I wouldn't even mention it. Just leave it there and watch his face through the window.

But there, perched on the corner of the hearth, about two feet from the electric fire, was a plate. My plate. Exactly as I had left it on the table, except that the gravy had now shrunk to a thin, rubbery brown skin around the remains of the lamb chop. The boiled potato had gone grey at the edges and the peas had sunken and dried.

So that was to be the deal. Clean my plate and I would get the car. Apparently, Warrel Blubb wasn't going to be the only one to eat shit.

Apple Crumble

Snow has fallen upon deep snow. The sky, lavender, grey and deep scarlet-rose, is heavy with more. Cars, barely one every half-hour, make their way slowly home, their tyres crunching on the freezing snow. The white boulder I rolled yesterday and left on the grass verge shines amber under the street lamp. My mittens are stiff. My face numb. Everything glistens.

There are shouts from the boys up the road firing snowballs at one another. I am playing alone, about a hundred yards away from them. My mother is watching me through the dining-room window. She looks worried. I am the proprietor of an imaginary cheese shop, carving slices of Cheddar from the huge rock of snow lit by the street lamp. As I ask my next customer what they want, I catch my mother's eye. I smile and wave at her and she looks down, embarrassed. The front door opens and she calls to me.

'It's time to come in now.'

'Oh, can't I stay out just a bit longer? There's a queue.'

'You must be freezing, you've been out there for hours. Anyway, it'll be dark soon.'

'Were you watching for Daddy?'

'No, I was watching you. What game were you playing?'

'Grocers. I've been selling cheese like Percy Salt does in his shop.'

She comes out and looks anxiously up the road at the boys having fun, yelling and running and sliding in the snow. Five of them, four from my own class. She looks disappointed. A cold little smile. She puts her arm round me, wincing at the frozen hairs on my cold duffel coat.

'Come on in, I've made a crumble.'

Even bad crumble is good. The perfect one is that whose juices have bubbled up through the pale rubble of the crust, staining it deep claret or gold. The ultimate is that which has damsons or greengages underneath and comes with a jug of yellow cream.

We chip away at the dry, gritty powder that fills the top third of the Pyrex baking dish. Sweet sawdust. The apples below have fallen into a watery mush. They are our own Bramleys from one of the three trees in the garden, which have been stored, wrapped in pages from the *Telegraph*, in a sack in the garage since September. Mother throws half the apple away when she peels it. She cuts in short thick strokes, as if she was cutting chips instead of paring the delicate skin from a fruit. She cooks the apples first, with a heaped spoon of white sugar and another of water, until they are starting to froth. Then she tips them into the dish. She takes down the yellow drum of Lion brand cloves from the shelf in the pantry, prises off the rusty lid and takes out two little stalks. These she tucks deep into the apple. Then she rubs the butter into the flour until it looks like dry breadcrumbs, and stirs in the sugar. This is tipped on to the apple and then the whole thing is put in the cool oven of the Aga.

The juice of Mother's crumble never bubbles up through its crust. The rough, uneven pebbles so vital for a perfect crumble are, in her version, as fine as sand. They are deep beige, almost the colour of a digestive biscuit. The bottom inch of crumble is sodden with apple juice. There is no cream, no custard.

Even bad crumble is good.

Sherbet Fountains

I never bought bags of sweets. They carried an implication that they were to be shared. A Mars bar or Milky Way carried no such baggage, and so that was what I bought with my pocket money.

A good way round sharing was to buy Sherbet Fountains – those tubes of acidic white powder wrapped in red-and-yellow paper with a stick of liquorice poked down the centre. You dipped the liquorice into the sherbet and sucked it. Not only did its staggeringly acid sweetness make your eyes water, you could have it all to yourself. At least I did. No one ever asked to suck my liquorice.

For some reason Sherbet Fountains were considered girls' stuff. Like Refreshers and Love Hearts. Nobody told me this until I had been seen dipping my little black stick into the depths of the fountain every day for a month or more. Real boys didn't eat Sherbet Fountains.

The only sweets I offered round were Love Hearts. Love Hearts were real girly sweets. Everyone knew that. But they could be very useful. I am sure I wasn't the only one to cunningly rearrange the sweeties in their packet so that, when I offered them round, the message – You're Cute, Kiss Me, Big Boy, etc. – got to the one intended. Invariably, my carefully constructed plan would misfire. There was always someone who would screw it up by taking two.

Radishes

Josh is showing me how to grow radishes in a corner of the garden that my father says is mine. Last year I planted cosmos, pink, white and deep-red daisies that danced on fine stems, and Indian Prince marigolds that had simple, single flowers and floppy leaves. Josh has raked away the tangle of their dried stems and seed heads, dumped them on the compost heap and raked the soil flat. He opens up the packet of seeds and passes them over to me. I empty them out into my hands and sprinkle them in long lines, but the seeds are so small they are dropping in tiny heaps.

'There's too many seeds and they're a bit too close together but we can thin them out when they come up,' says Josh.

Two weeks later some of the seeds have germinated, I am lying on my stomach on the grass looking at the baby leaves that have come up, a mixture of gaps and tufty bunches. I hear Josh's bike in the drive and then the garage doors rattling open. I sit there gazing at the leaves for a minute or two then walk over to the garage. Josh is getting changed. His denim jacket is on the seat of his Triumph, and he is just undoing his belt. Josh's white-T shirt is out of shape and so short it barely comes down to his belly button. It looks like he's had it for years. Mum would have thrown mine out before it got like that. He pulls his jeans off and lays them over the bike. He is standing there in nothing but his T-shirt. Josh never seems to wear any underwear. He walks round to the back of his bike and takes a pair of thin, faded shorts out of the shiny black box on the back and pulls them on, then, without putting on any shoes, he picks me up in his arms and we jog out to the garden.

'Come and see my radishes, they're huge,' I say, exaggerating slightly.

Josh pulls a set of leaves gently between his thumb and fingers. At the end of the thin stem is a tiny pink radish, just big enough to be recognisable. 'Eat it, go on,' he urges. The little root is crunchy, hot, mustardy, exciting, like my mouth is on fire. I don't know whether I like it or not. Josh laughs and starts picking out many more of the seedlings. He clasps them in his hand and takes them back to his bike, where he puts them in a little plastic bag and lays them gently in the black box on the back of his bike. 'They're for my salad,' he says. Holding them gently, protectively, as you might a baby bird.

This week we have picked about twenty radishes, long, thin ones with white tips and fuschia-pink skins, the insides as crisp and white as baby's teeth. I am still not sure if I like them or not but Dad seems to. He sort of wells up when I give them to him. 'Go on, eat them then,' I plead.

'Later.'

When we found the radishes in the fridge a week later, shrivelled, bendy, their leaves yellow, I am not sure who was more upset, Josh or me. Dad hadn't really been in the house much, and I forgot to tell Mum they were there. After that I didn't really pick any more. I told Josh he could have them all but he didn't seem to want them either.

Having people to do both the garden and the housework was unusual round our way. Most of our neighbours either mowed their back lawns and dug their vegetable patches, though some had wild gardens, rough lawn with overgrown brambles and purple loosestrife at the far end. Front gardens, on the other hand, were always tidy and smart. An orderly mix of heather, conifers and privet hedges. The Marks & Spencer's grey suit of gardens. In summer, white alyssum was kept in pert balls and gentian-blue lobelia trailed gently along the edge of immaculate lawns no bigger than a duvet. Purple aubrietia was pruned into neat nests that cascaded from rockery walls. A dog turd would have been cleaned up before it was barely cold.

No one in our road was unemployed, save gruff old Mr Manley, who was as old as God and looked rather like Monet, and Mr Saunders, who had hurt his leg at work and now spent his day practising the clarinet. Few, if any, of the women worked. Everyone had children of more or less the same age but the parents all seemed so old, with everyone in their forties and fifties. There were no babies, no single mothers, no young, childless couples. No blacks, no homosexuals, no foreigners. The only pets were our Labrador, Mr Manley's black Scottie and a few assorted guinea pigs and hamsters. I think the Butlers had a tabby cat. Neat, calm, polite, distant, with only the children ever setting foot in one another's houses.

One day I came in cold and wet through. My short trousers stuck to my legs and my socks had worked their way down to my ankles. My feet squidged in my sandals as I walked. Josh grabbed his towel. 'You're soaked,' he laughed. 'Come on, let's get you into some dry clothes.' He followed me upstairs and he pulled my T-shirt up over my head, then slid my shorts and little white Y-front pants down. He rubbed me all over with the towel, growling like a tiger, tickling me till I couldn't stop laughing. Josh dried my arms, making me hold them high above my head, and then my legs, which were shivering and covered in little white pimples. He dried my thighs and then held my cold, wet dick in his right hand, stroking it dry with his towel, tenderly, protectively, like he was holding a frightened mouse.

Tinned Fruit

We lived in a world of tinned fruit. There were tinned peaches for high days and holidays, fruit cocktail for every-day and tinned pears for my father who said they were better than fresh. There were apricots and segments of mandarin oranges that turned up in orange jelly and, once, figs, which nobody really liked. On one occasion we tried mango but my father said it tasted fishy. I wasn't allowed to try. 'You won't like it.'

The highlight was not the peaches that we ate when someone special came to tea, but the diced delights of fruit cocktail. Grey cubes of grainy pear, semi-cubes of peach, ridged chunks of pineapple and, best of all, lipstick-red maraschino cherries all floating in a divinely sweet syrup. We ate it from red Pyrex dishes, the fruit poking up like a multicoloured rockery in a pool of Ideal milk.

'If you really want to, dear,' was my mother's answer for anything I wanted to do that she would rather I didn't. This was her stock answer to my question: Can I make a fruit sundae? By make I meant assemble. My fruit sundae was a gloriously over-the-top mess of strawberry ice cream, tinned fruit cocktail, maraschino cherries and any nuts I could lay my hands on. I always saved a cherry for the centre. Believe me when I tell you it was the envy of all who set eyes upon it.

Lamb Chop

Sometimes I would come home at lunchtime to find my mother in her bedroom, curtains drawn. If I listened at the crack in the door I could hear her breathing, slow, peaceful breaths with a slight rasp coming from somewhere deep in her chest. On those days Mum, Mrs Poole, who knows who, would set out something for my lunch: ham salad; cold roast pork with pickled walnuts and crackling; a Birds Eye Chicken Pie ready to go into the oven; cold roast beef and salad. I didn't enquire about the provenance of these meals. They just appeared and I ate them and that was that.

One day I came home at lunchtime to find my mother had done chops and peas. It was her knee-jerk meal. When she was late back from the shops, her green Beetle with dented left wing still warm on the drive, the chops would be juicy with the thinnest line of pink running through their middle. If she had got started early I might as well be eating the sole of my father's brown brogues.

That day the chops were moist and sweet, a thin crust from the frying pan on their edges and fat the colour of amber. There was a bone to chew, tantalisingly browned. Best of all she had done little roast potatoes just for me. OK, so they didn't have the gorgeous benefit of being cooked round the roast but they were still scrunchy round the edges, fluffy inside and so hot I had to jiggle them round my mouth so they didn't burn my tongue.

'I'm sorry, darling,' she said, rubbing softly at an imaginary stain on the kitchen table, 'but I think you're going to have to stay for school dinners. It's just a bit too much for me at the moment. As soon as I'm better you can come back home again. I'm sorry, lamb chop.'

It was like she had just taken out a gun and shot me.

Tapioca

'No thank you,' I say to the tight-lipped prefect who is ladling great splodges of ivory-grey tapioca into shallow bowls and passing them round the table, 'I'm full.' Her eyes narrow and one corner of her mouth turns up. 'Sorry, you have to eat it, it's the rules.' The guy opposite me, who smells like digestive biscuits and I think lives on the council estate I am not allowed to go to, is wolfing his down like it was warm treacle sponge or trifle, or maybe chocolate sponge pudding. But it's not. This is the most vile thing I have ever put in my mouth, like someone has stirred frog-spawn into wallpaper paste. Like porridge with bogeys in it. Like something an old man has hockled up into his hanky.

When I get home I am going to tell Mum to write a note letting me off this stuff. The stew wasn't that bad, apart from the swedes which were bitter and something flabby that could have been fat but felt more like a big fat slug. I spread the spittle-coloured glue around my dish right up the sides in the hope I will have to eat less of it. 'You must show me your bowls before you leave the table,' says Tight Lips, 'They must be clean, otherwise you'll be here all afternoon.'

Considering we have an outdoor PE lesson this after-noon, staying in the warm, playing with a bowl of rice doesn't seem such a bad option. At home, going without pudding is a punishment, at school eating it is. Yesterday's sponge with bright red jam and desiccated coconut wasn't so bad, neither was the chocolate blancmange with pretend cream and hundreds and thousands on it. But this is dis-gusting. Everyone has finished and is waiting for me, glar-ing at me, wanting to go out and play. 'Oh, hurry up, will you, I've got netball practice,' says Tight Lips. And so, with that I push my bowl and spoon over to the Digestive Biscuit guy and say, 'You eat it.' He glances furtively at Little Miss Netball Practice, who nods a mean little nod and the evil stuff was gone quicker than you could sneeze.

And so that was it. Over the next few weeks Digestive Biscuit boy hoovered up egg-and-bacon flan, tomato flan, liver and cabbage, liver and mashed swede, mince with carrots, mince with boiled marrow, something-I'm-not-quite-sure-of-in-white-sauce, pink blancmange with very thick skin on it, yellow blancmange with very thick skin on it, gravy with a very thick skin on it and chocolate semolina which even he said looked like something that had come out of a baby's arse.

Treacle Tart

Not everything ended up on Digestive Biscuit boy's plate. Nothing would have got me to part with jam tart with its thick crumbly pastry and thin layer of raspberry jam, or rhubarb sponge, or for that matter shepherd's pie, fish pie, cheese pie, cottage pie, faggots, fish and chips, sausage hotpot, Irish stew or anything remotely connected to potatoes. The real treasure, though, was the treacle tart that came in a shallow aluminium tray, its golden layer of breadcrumbs and golden syrup criss-crossed with ribbons of curly pastry with a jug of custard at its side.

For all its golden syrup school treacle tart wasn't that sweet. It was slightly dry and stuck to your spoon so hard you had to scrape it off your teeth. What appealed was the pastry, not so much the taste but the feel of it. Pale pastry that crumbled in your mouth then coated it with crumbs and fat. Together with the crumbs and syrup, this was the most sublime texture I had ever had in my mouth. Better, even, than Mother's flapjacks, Father's trifle. Almost as sublime as toast.

Crumpets

'Come on, put your shoes on, we're going for a walk.'

We never go for a walk.

Penn Common is a rolling meadow of tall bracken, moss and the odd thicket of birch trees. In spring there are primroses and in autumn mushrooms. Right now there is just a cold east wind and fine needles of rain. My ears are pink. My mother keeps clapping her hands over hers. We never do anything like this.

I am dawdling twenty feet behind them, catching the odd word here and there. 'Not in hospital, at home ...' 'Please, please let me be at home ...', '... be able to cope ...', 'If he was only tougher ...'

My father bends his head. 'If the worst comes to the worst ...', '... taken into care, it's not like it used to be.'

I guess my mother is pregnant, that she doesn't want to have the baby in hospital and that for some reason it may have to go into care. I rather fancy the idea of a little brother or perhaps a sister.

We walk on, my face getting so cold and numb I can barely feel my tongue. We keep walking, and now both of them have their heads bent down against the stinging rain. My father puts his arm around my mother. He has never done this before. Perhaps she's cold. I think they are crying. Not once do they look back at me.

At home my father tears open a packet of crumpets and toasts them on the Aga. He puts so much butter on them that it runs through the holes and down our arms as we pull at the soft, warm dough with our teeth. We all run our fingers round our plates and lick the stray butter off them. Everyone is so quiet. Both of them have red eyes like white rabbits. I thought everyone was happy when you were having a baby.

Bubblegum

Lunch was a turnstile you went through to get your pocket money. 'Can I get down now?' was followed by a coy smile, head cocked to my left, my right leg scuffing gently at the black linoleum of the kitchen floor. If this offensive didn't work, 'Daddy,' long pause, 'haven't you forgotten something?' was usually enough to extract a sixpenny piece from his trouser pocket.

A sixpence meant bubblegum. To be more precise it meant three packets of Beatlecards or two packets of Beatlecards and a Sherbet Fountain. I am not sure if the card photographs of John, Paul, George and Ringo smelled of bubblegum, or if the bubblegum smelled of cardboard. I was never an avid collector and used them as cash at school. What mattered was the flat, rose-pink piece of bubblegum and its smooth surface, the art of unwrapping the thin paper round it and my ability to put the entire sheet of gum in my mouth in one go.

My ability to fart was matched only by my expertise in blowing 'Beatlegum' into pink balloons the size of a tennis ball. Balloons whose only point was to burst and stick to your top lip and right cheek. The day I got the hang of bubble-blowing I raced home armed with three sheets of gum. My mother was sitting on a chair, her right hand clutching her chest and looking down at her lap. I burst in and kneeled down in front of her, taking huge breaths and blowing my bubblegum into a transparent pink globe less than six inches from her face. Her eyes were closed and she had a white lace-edged handkerchief in her left hand.

My father walked in just as my bubble burst. 'Sometimes you are so thoughtless. Now leave her in peace,' he snapped while my mother sat, motionless except for a heaving chest, gasping for breath.

Porridge

There were only two breakfast cereals I would eat: Sugar Puffs and Cap'n Crunch. Weetabix, Alpen, Shredded Wheat, Rice Krispies, Corn Flakes and Coco Pops all fell at the first post because they needed milk on them. Eating a Shredded Wheat without a soaking of milk is like one of those party games you play when you're drunk. Sugar Puffs and Cap'n Crunch were quite palatable eaten dry and so that was breakfast. Every single day. It didn't occur to me that those cereals were only edible without milk because they were so sweet. You can swallow pretty much anything if it comes with a dose of sugar.

Today Dad makes my breakfast. Hot Ribena and porridge with sugar.

'Where's Mum?'

'She's upstairs, she's getting up late today.'

Mum never gets up late. Must be something to do with her being pregnant. Don't know why no one has told me about it yet. I mean, this is going to make a big difference to my life. Having a brother or sister could turn my world upside down. Especially if I don't like them.

I don't want porridge. You can't eat it because it's so hot. Then you can't eat it because it's so cold. The difference between the two is barely three minutes. When you catch porridge at the right moment it is like being wrapped in a cashmere blanket. A food so comforting and soul-warming you imagine there is no problem on earth it could not solve. And then, when you are halfway through the bowl, it cools. The last two or three spoonfuls make me gag. If I put enough sugar on it I can just about get it down, though one day I swear the whole lot will come back up through my nose.

My father interferes with what I eat more than anyone else. The rule is simple: for breakfast I have dry cereal and Tree Top orange squash. Yet he makes me eat this pap called porridge and insists I have a glass of Ribena. Then he tries to get me to drink tea. Nothing, but nothing will get me to drink tea. Even with sugar in it.

Every time my dad feeds me he goes quiet, thoughtful, distant even. This big man bites his bottom lip and gazes intently at my skinny arms and spindly legs. He watches, silently, at the way I pick at my food, pushing it round the plate when I don't like it. Pulling a face. My father's disappointment in his youngest son is so obvious you could put it on a plate and eat it.

The Day the Gardener Came

The one man to whom I wasn't a disappointment was Josh. I loved every moment he was around and would stand at his side as he cleaned the pond of its green duckweed, tugged dandelions from the lawn and snipped the dead-heads off Dad's prized dahlias. He didn't do the lawn. Mowing the lawn in wide, green stripes was Dad's job, marching up and down its great length with the smell of oil and cut grass trailing behind him. The gardening equivalent of carving the turkey. It said, 'I'm in charge.'

Where my father was cold, Josh was warm. Where Dad would tell me to get down, Josh would pick me up. He would sit me on his lap, bounce me on his shoulders, and sit and talk to me in the garage long after he had finished tying up the honeysuckle or raking the leaves from the lawn. Sometimes I would paint pictures for him, my much practised wishy-washy watercolours of heather-covered hills and window ledges with potted plants on them. He would put them away carefully in his empty lunch box, like they were fragile, ancient parchments and take them home.

If I walked in when Josh was getting changed he'd instantly stop and talk to me, sometimes wearing nothing at all. He started bringing magazines, the two of us straddling the wide seat of his motorbike, him sitting behind me with his arms hugged around me, slowly turning the pages for me. He said it was probably best not to tell anyone about the magazines.

One day I ran into Mum and Dad's bedroom to ask Dad if I could go out and play. Dad hadn't got any clothes on and got cross and told me to knock on the door next time. I told him that Josh never minded when I saw him naked. Mum and Dad glanced across at one another, then Dad looked back down at the floor.

The following week I ran home from school to see Josh as usual. His motorbike wasn't there, and in the garden was a wiry old man bending over the rose beds, a wheelbarrow full of weeds at his side. 'Who are you?' I demanded, glaring at him, my bottom lip starting to quiver.

'Be away with you,' he snapped. 'Can't you see I'm busy?'

Hot Chocolate 1

Nine years old and I still cannot swim without a rubber ring. There are four of us, all boys, who occupy the non-swimmers' end of the pool each Wednesday afternoon. As if this isn't humiliation enough, the rubber rings are pink and yellow.

The changing rooms are an ordeal. Mr Staley allows us barely five minutes to get dried and back into our white pants, grey shirts and black trousers. We are allowed to put our ties on in the coach. The changing cubicles are freezing and so crowded it is impossible to dry yourself thoroughly. We all dry one another's backs. Even though there is no room to stretch a towel I brace myself for the crack of a wet one being flicked at my matchstick legs. Sometimes you get your pants thrown out on to the wet deck, necessitating a mad, naked dash to retrieve them. We flick each other's cold, wet ears, wring our sodden trunks in one another's shoes, make grabs at each other's cocks. On the bus back our wet hair drips down our backs, and the carpet-covered seats make us itch all the way home.

Before we board the coach, we meet up with the girls in the concourse. The tall echoing room smells of bleach and hot chocolate. No one gets tea or coffee from the machine, only chocolate, which is thin and hot with a swirl of pinky-brown froth on top. We clutch at the plastic cups to warm our hands. Even in summer my teeth chatter.

This may be just colouring and sugar, it may never have seen a cocoa pod, but it is the drink I wait for all week. First sip, too hot; my top lip stings, a pink pimple instantly swells in the centre. I poke my tongue into the thin plastic cup and scoop up a trace of froth. Within a minute, maybe less if the room is icy, though still too hot to drink, the cocoa is cool enough to sip. Each mouthful hurts as it goes down. Like I am swallowing a gobstopper.

Hot Chocolate 2

My aunt turns the heat off just before the milk boils. She catches it exactly at the point at which the milk will still come to the boil but will stop rising before it goes over the edge of the pan. After thirty years in the same house she has the procedure down to a fine art. I don't, and manage to either make lukewarm cocoa or spend ten minutes mopping up the boiled-over milk. Not that it would matter, if it wasn't for the pervasive smell and for the fact that milk sticks to an electric ring much like airplane glue sticks to balsa wood.

The worst thing about making cocoa for my aunt is having to use her foul sterilised milk. My father calls it buggerised milk. You can tell how nasty this stuff is by the fact that it doesn't need to go in the fridge – how weird is that? It has been boiled during processing so when you make cocoa it has effectively been boiled twice. No wonder it tastes like old people smell.

Milk Skin

Skin. Even the word sends shivers down my spine. This is the stuff that you peel off your chest when you have sunburn; it's the little flap left hanging when you cut yourself that catches on everything; it's the transparent sheath left behind by an emerging snake. Skin is the word I link automatically with grazed shins or something mummified. So what is it doing floating on my cocoa?

You either like the thin layer of wrinkled skin that forms on hot milk or you don't. This is something you cannot not mind about. It has to be love or utter loathing. I hate milk skin most when it is only half formed, so that you can barely see it, so you sip it by mistake and it ends up hanging from your top lip.

Worst of all is when someone 'stirs it in' so that you get lots of little flakes that catch on your tongue and you have to remove with finger and thumb. If I'm quick enough I catch the layer that forms on cocoa and milky coffee just as it is thick enough to come off in one piece. Then it sticks round the teaspoon like melted cling film.

Jammie Dodgers

Minnie Blubb kept a clean house. You took your shoes off at
the door and stepped over rather than on the shocking-pink
fluffy doormat. You prayed your stockinged feet didn't
leave sweatprints on the polished vinyl tiles. At the Blubbs
you learned to walk on air. I stopped off there every day
on the way back from school with Warrel, the adored son
of Minnie and Arthur Blubb.

Warrel was a boy brought up in cotton wool. The house
was always warm, his slippers waited patiently by the door
for when he came home. His blazer was always brushed.
His mother even combed his hair for him. In return he had
to wash his hands before he sat at the table. He was smug,
arrogant, stubborn, boastful, impatient and ugly. He was
my best friend. We walked to school together, sat together,
walked back home together for lunch, walked back to
school, sat together, walked back home together again. We
played together, did our homework together, went to Sunday school together. I couldn't even bear to be away from
him while he had his tea. I would sit at the table with him,
watching him devour every mouthful.

Minnie Blubb would sit on one side of Warrel, me
the other. She hung on her precious son's every word, I
hung on his every mouthful. Mrs Blubb never offered me
so much as a biscuit. Warrel's teas were a schoolboy's
dream. No chops and congealed gravy for this boy; just

spaghetti in tomato sauce, fish fingers or sausages and chips.

Every one of Warrel's teas ended with a plate of biscuits and cake. There were chocolate chip cookies and Cadbury's Fingers, Jammie Dodgers, Bourbon biscuits and Jaffa Cakes, slices of home-made Victoria sponge and chocolate digestives. At Christmas there would be a mince pie. He would pick up each biscuit and roll it over and over, examining it, slowly contemplating its sweet symmetry. Sometimes there was a Tunnock's wafer or (bastard) a chocolate marshmallow teacake in its red-and-silver foil. There was milk shake too, strawberry flavour and with a straw. A straw.

His big, yellow buck teeth nibbled through each plateful like a squirrel at a bag of mixed nuts. He savoured every crumb. He would nibble away the top layer of each Bourbon biscuit, then slowly lick off the rectangle of chocolate cream below. Sometimes he would play airplanes with a Jammie Dodger, flying it within half an inch of my nose and making yyyyyoooowwmm airplane noises before slipping it whole into his mouth. 'OK, I've finished, we can go out and play now.'

Peach Flan

Mrs Muggeridge was a short, solid, black woman. It wasn't her skin that was black, it was her soul. In the six weeks she spent as our cleaner she never smiled once. She would shoo me away like a pesky fly. A woman steeped in vinegar. A hairy mole on her chin did her no favours.

Mrs Muggeridge was more than a cleaner. When my mother was in bed, too weak to cook, she would make lunch for me. If ever there was a meal seasoned with hatred this was it. Hatred for a life that saw her scrubbing people's lavatories for a living; hatred for having to feed a fussy little boy when she could have none of her own; hatred for the sirloin steak she grilled for my Monday lunches while she would go home to boiled neck of fatty lamb and carrots.

We never found out her Christian name. I'm not sure she even had one. It wouldn't surprise me if she had been christened Mrs Muggeridge. For all this, her cooking had a spring in its step. Her peas were green not grey, her pork chops were not brown and dry like Mother's but salty outside and juicy within. Her flapjacks were soft and crumbly not brittle. On Fridays she would make a fruit flan – tinned peaches and a cocktail cherry on a yellow sponge base.

One morning when I was off school with one of the bilious attacks that came so conveniently before maths tests, she showed me how to make the peach flan. The sponge base came from a packet, the peaches from a tin. But she let me arrange the slices in the sponge case, neatly over-lapping one on another. She produced the cherry from a tissue in her apron pocket. I put it exactly in the centre. We opened a sachet of Quick-Gel and mixed it with hot water. As soon as the red gunge started to cool I spooned it over the fruit. It set in seconds. There it was, a great orange and red wheel. I wanted to take it upstairs to show my mother but Mrs Muggeridge wouldn't let me. The wait for my father to come home for lunch was interminable. I wanted to see his face when he saw what I'd made.

'Don't be nosy,' she snapped when I asked her what her husband did, trying to fill a silence. 'He isn't around any more. I've had to do without him for a year now. Just like you are going to have to do without your mother.'

That night, as he was tucking me into bed, I asked my father what she meant by 'just like you are going to have to'.

I never saw Mrs Muggeridge or her peach flan again.

Mince Pies 1

'Isn't it a bit early?' I say, quizzing Mum over her plan to make the mince pies ten days before Christmas.

'No, I'm going to put them in the freezer so they are ready for you to pop in the oven whenever you want one.' It's about time we had something in the freezer.

Mum is getting shorter, her back seems arched now, as if she's carrying coal and her eyes are tired, spent. Two years ago she was tall, willowy, upright; now it seems like an effort for her to stand. 'Get the rolling pin out, let's get them done.'

The patty tins are rusty, with a faint layer of grease in

the bottom of each hollow. I wipe them out with a piece of kitchen paper. I love making pastry, bringing my hands high up in the air as I rub the tiny cubes of cold butter and soft lard into the flour. It's an exaggerated action, but one that gets the air into the pastry and makes it light. We add water, but no sugar, no egg, and pull the ingredients into a small boulder. 'I thought we were supposed to let it rest, Mum,' I chime in, a trick I had read in a magazine of hers.

Mum starts to roll the pastry out, concentrating hard, like every push is a piece of mathematics. 'Here, you have a go, darling.' She hands me the wooden pin with its red handles and goes to the top drawer for one of her Ventolin inhalers. There seem to be more than ever lately. I found one in the map pocket of the car yesterday. She sits down on a kitchen stool, the one with the leg that wobbles, and puts the inhaler to her mouth. She closes her eyes and presses the top down. She calls it her 'puffer'. Every time she presses it down, she seems to jump, like she has been punched in the chest.

I continue rolling the pastry, a wiggly-edged rectangle that looks like a map of Australia. A piece falls off. New Zealand, I suppose. We have a set of red plastic tart cutters with crinkle edges, but only ever use one of them. I cut out almost two dozen over the next ten minutes, rolling and stretching where I must, patching a hole, a tear, a crack. I push the pastry down loosely into the patty tins. I don't want the pastry to stick. Mum walks over to the larder and there is much clanking and banging, I hear tins being pushed along the shelves, even the Christmas puddings being moved.

'Sorry, honeypie, I could have sworn I had some mince-meat, we'll have to put it all away in the fridge till tomorrow.'

Mince Pies 2

'But Mummy, you PROMISED!'

'Darling, I'm sorry, I forgot to get it when I went to the shops.'

'You're HOPELESS, I hope you DIE.' I run up the stairs to my room, slam the door and lie face down on the bed. I knew she'd forget. I just KNEW it.

The Night Just Before Christmas

It is a couple of nights before Christmas, about five-thirty in the morning, and I'm snuggled down under the sheets. I'm warm in my striped winceyette pyjamas and soft cotton bedding, my bedspread pulled up tight around my ears. Toasty. Outside, the thick frost still twinkles under the street lights. Deep silence. There are flakes of frost around the edges of the glass in the bedroom window. I can feel my warm breath on the back of my hand.

If I stretch my feet out, right down to the bottom of the bed, I can, with pointy toes, feel a heavy weight. Something told me Santa Claus would come early this year. What with Mummy so desperately poorly – I heard the doctor say something about oxygen tanks last night and my father kept holding his forehead in his hand, his thumb pressing on his right temple – and everyone looking so miserable, he knew we all needed cheering up. This means I get my presents before anyone else, and the ones under the tree can wait till after Christmas lunch.

My Christmas stocking is actually a cotton pillowcase. Father Christmas always leaves it at the bottom of the bed. Last year there was a cuckoo clock and a sort of glass globe with metal paddles inside that went round in the sun but stopped as soon as it got dark. There was a Spirograph, a green MG convertible for my Scalextrics track, more Lego and Meccano pieces, a string frog puppet, a set of short coloured chalks which I loved and a pair of football boots which I didn't. The boots had blue plastic studs. No one else at school had boots with blue plastic studs. Just me. They sounded like high heels when you walked in them. David Woodford laughed at them. Maxwell Mallin laughed at them. This year I'm hoping for my own copy of *A Hard Day's Night* and a pair of Hush Puppies. The brown suede ones with the black elastic on the side like Adrian's.

I push back the bedspread and the warm cocoon of brushed cotton sheets. There is no bulging sack and casual scattering of beribboned boxes. No round lump of clementine in the far corner of the pillowcase, no Cadbury's Selection box in the shape of a sock. Just Daddy, kneeling, his elbows resting on the bed, his head in his hands. Sobbing. He climbs further on to the bed and wraps his arms tightly round me. I bury my face in his soft Viyella check shirt.

Marshmallows

I didn't go to the funeral. I didn't even know it was happening. My brother drove me to Birmingham in his minivan to stay with my aunt and uncle and that was that.

My aunt's house was neat, formal, always quiet, and now, with the curtains drawn, exceptionally so. Everyone, my uncle, visiting neighbours, the doctor's family who lived next door, would creep around, speaking in voices so low as to be almost a whisper. Meals – tinned tomato soup, lamb chops with mint sauce, Bisto gravy and sliced green beans – were eaten in silence. Not a word. When I said 'thank you' or 'yes, please' in a cheery voice, everyone looked down at the floor like I was committing some terrible *faux pas*.

Two days later my brother collected me and we drove back home. My aunt held a lace-edged hanky to her mouth as she waved goodbye. My father took me upstairs and left me to get ready for bed. 'I'll be up soon to tuck you in.' Apart from those last few nights before she died, this was to be the first time in a year or more that my mother had failed to come in and kiss me good night.

As I snuggled down deep into my bed I saw two white marshmallows on my bedside table. I had never been allowed to eat in bed and when my father came upstairs I asked if they were for me. 'Of course they are, I know they're your favourites.' They weren't, and he knew it, but I had, in a school essay written shortly before my mother's death, described them as being the nearest food to a kiss. Soft, sweet, tender, pink. True, I had said I didn't like the pink ones but I didn't really mean it. They all tasted the same anyway.

Each night for the next two years I found two, sometimes three fluffy, sugary marshmallows on my bedside table. It was the good night kiss I missed more than anything, more than her hugs, her cuddles, her whispered 'Night-night, sleep tight.' No Walnut Whip, no Cadbury's Flake, no sugared almond could ever replace that kiss. I'm not sure a marshmallow really came that close.

Fried Eggs

My father had never read Proust, but he did have a collection of mock-leather-bound classics he bought from an advertisement in the *Daily Telegraph*. His pipe and his subscription to the *Reader's Digest* and *National Geographic* gave him the air of man who was well read. He knew things.

So when he clicked that he had a sporty son who ate eggs and a spotty one who didn't he knew exactly what to think.

It was quite obvious that to turn an nine-year-old nancy boy (his phrase) into a strapping son-to-be-proud-of you simply added an egg. Boiled, fried, scrambled, poached it mattered not. Neither did it matter that the nancy boy had thrown up every egg he had ever tried to swallow. Eggs, according to my father, maketh the man.

If he had any doubts about his diagnosis, the Egg Marketing Board settled them. Their television campaign showed a sweet, cheeky blond boy cracking open his breakfast egg to the pleasure of his Aunt Het. Just the sort of lad my father would have loved me to be.

For years my mother had been lying for me. Easy when I had my tea before her husband arrived home. According to her, I had wolfed two boiled eggs or a pair of poached eggs on toast. I had asked for seconds of scrambled eggs and even tackled, though not quite finished, a fried egg. He never doubted her for one second. Or, more likely, he never considered her capable of lying to him.

It would sit there quivering; the food from hell. The white to make you gag. The yolk to make you retch. As the minutes ticked away the skin on the yolk would thicken then shrink. By the time the bacon and sausage had been eaten (slowly, anything to delay the inevitable) a dimple had started to form in the centre of the yolk. If you pressed your fork in it, the hardening yellow stuck to it like fudge.

Leaving the egg till last gave several windows of opportunity. The end of the world; the dog jumping on my lap and wolfing the offending item from my plate; or my father having a change of heart, taking pity on his poor struggling son and allowing him to get down from the table. There was also the possibility of my prayers being answered – the most usual one being that he might drop dead.

What actually happened was that the egg simply congealed and became even harder to swallow. I would slouch over the table as if I was about to collapse, pushing at the fried egg with my fork, slowly putting pressure on the dome of yolk with the prongs of the fork, just stopping short of breaking the skin and revealing the thickening ovum.

The horror of eggs for breakfast started a good hour or more before getting to the table. It started the second I woke on a Sunday morning to the smell of wet bacon spitting in the charred black frying pan and the sharp sting of grilled tomatoes coming up the stairs. By lying in bed until I heard his footsteps on the treads I could work myself up into a right state, so that by the time I was told 'put your dressing gown on, I've made you some breakfast' I would be feeling ill, queasy, angry, frustrated, sick all at the same time. By the time I had come down the stairs one by one I had worked myself up into one of my notorious bilious attacks.

'You can't eat nothing for breakfast, you'll faint.' I tried, for the hundredth time, to tell him I didn't like eggs, they made me feel poorly. 'Of course you like eggs, everyone likes eggs. You always ate them before.' His 'before' meaning not so much when my mother was alive but before he had to cook, wash up and look after me. 'And if you won't eat them on your own, I'll make you eat them,' he threatened. Cold, dry, unyielding.

Smelling it and hearing it sputter in the pan was bad enough. Setting eyes on the one-eyed yellow monster was a moment of deep anxiety, like seeing a squashed hedgehog on the road. Except that this time I didn't want to look even for a second.

Something worried my father about the Sunday ritual of feeding eggs to his egg-hating son. His brow wrinkled and his eyes narrowed as if what he was doing to his son truly pained him. My mother had never forced me to eat anything in her life. He cut the egg into small pieces, now as hard as toffee. He held me by the shoulder. He told me to open my mouth or he would hit me. He shook almost as much as I did. The sulphurous smell of the egg made me gag. I shuddered and shook my head from side to side. As the egg on the fork got near to my closed lips I threw my head fast from left to right. The fork went flying. The egg hit first the table then the floor. I was crying. Snot hit my top lip. I felt something coming up into my mouth from my stomach. Something burning and vile. I pushed my chair back and ran upstairs to the bathroom, my face smeared with tears and egg and snot and vomit.

Cheese on Toast

I am not sure the cooking is any worse since Mum died. But it isn't much better either. Dad does at least make cheese on toast for me. Weird the way he does it, though, grating the Cracker Barrel into a small pan of melted butter, stirring it round until it melts, then pouring it over the hot toast. It's pretty good, apart from when he overcooks it and it goes chewy, like cheese-flavoured bubblegum. I once told him I could mend my bike tyres with it and he went very quiet. I wish I hadn't said it really.

What I like about it now is how moist it is, juicier than when Mum used to slice cheese and put it under the grill. She didn't use Cracker Barrel for that, though. Mum bought her cheese from Percy Salt, and would ask to taste it before he cut off a hunk from the great fat cheese on the shelf behind him. He used to wrap it in greaseproof and would always give me a little piece to taste. Sometimes it was really strong and all the veins on the roof of my mouth used to stand out. I don't think my Dad likes asking for things in the shop, he always picks food up ready-packed, even the bacon and the tea. And he buys tins of ham all the time now, instead of letting Mr Salt slice pieces off the big leg he keeps in the fridge. But his cheese on toast is better. Sometimes I think it's the best dinner in the world.

Cheese-and-Onion Crisps

On Saturdays Dad used to buy a crab and we would spend much of the afternoon taking it to pieces. We would spread yesterday's newspaper out on the table and then twist off the claws and legs. He would crack open the fat orange and black claws with his hammer and leave me to wheedle the flesh from the spindly legs. He always got more out than I did, and often in one fat piece. At about four in the afternoon, he would make crab-and-watercress sandwiches for us all, carefully keeping the white and brown crabmeat separate with the sprigs of watercress in between. It took about two hours to prepare the crab, twenty minutes to clean up the kitchen and retrieve all the bits of shrapnel that had shot all over the room, and barely five minutes to wolf the sandwiches.

After Mum died we never had crab again, nor any of Dad's favourite things like tripe and onions or liver and bacon or cauliflower cheese. He never cooked himself a kipper or made roast pork with crackling. I don't think he even cooked a steak, let alone had it with mushroom ketchup and crinkle-cut chips, which he loved. It was as if he couldn't bear to think about that stuff any more.

A few things didn't change. On Saturday mornings he would still peel four big mushrooms and cut off the stalks with his penknife, then put them in a transparent Pyrex dish with some butter, salt and a few shakes of mushroom ketchup. Covered with a lid they would cook slowly in the slow oven of the Aga till they were as soft as a bit of braised steak. He would then lift them on to a couple of rounds of hot toast and dribble the juices from the dish over the top.

Sitting alone at the vast empty kitchen table, tucking into his mushrooms on toast, he seemed so much smaller now – like he was wearing a coat that was too big for him.

I ate almost nothing at school. For the first six months after Mum died I lived on cheese-and-onion crisps and chocolate marshmallow 'teacakes' – the ones with the red-and-silver foil – bought with my dinner money. The nearest thing I had to a meal was the cheese on toast or spaghetti hoops Dad made when he came home in the evening. Heaven knows what Dad ate.

Fray Bentos Steak & Kidney Pie

We have started having chicken pies for tea. Eating a slice of pie is like being in love. Nothing Dad makes for tea – cheese on toast, spaghetti hoops, baked potatoes – is quite so comforting as having my own little pie. The pastry is soft and crumbling, the filling rich with dark brown gravy. The whole thing tender as a bruise. Sometimes we have steak and kidney instead, with frozen peas on the side and a knob of butter. Dad doesn't make the pies of course, they are Birds Eye, but that doesn't stop them being my favourite tea.

Everyone seems to be talking about another pie, a bigger

one, that comes in a tin and you cook it with its lid on. Dad seems reluctant to buy one, even though we have seen it advertised on the TV. He says he doesn't think I'll like it. A pie in a tin seems such a neat idea but I can tell he's not keen. I think he's scared it won't work out, like when he tried to make flapjacks and we couldn't get them out of the tin or when he made Heinz chocolate sponge pudding and it boiled dry.

'I think we've done something wrong,' mutters Dad, looking down at the deflated pie with its sodden, slimy pastry. 'Don't eat it if you don't want to.'

I have to eat it. I've been nagging for it for weeks. The filling smells like the food we put out for the dog, though in all fairness it tastes a whole lot better. The pastry is like a soggy dishcloth and smells like one too. I don't like to say that on TV the pastry is all puffed and crisp. I don't know what he's done wrong this time.

Smoked Haddock

I may have rolled the pastry for a mince pie or fingered the butter, flour and sugar crust for a crumble, but at nine years old I had yet to cook an entire meal. My cooking had been confined to things I could do unsupervised, safe things. So protective had my mother been of her son's precious fingers I had yet to turn an oven on or light the gas.

Next to the kitchen was a small scullery, a back-up

kitchen with a sink, a low-fangled cream Belling cooker and grill, a fridge whose door squeaked. It wasn't a room you could feel at home in, no heating and no room to move, but its existence kept the main kitchen free from potato peelings, the stink of grilled kippers on a Sunday morning and the dripping chaos of Mother's washing up. I could reach the controls of the oven, but lighting the grill meant standing on a stool or the creaking chrome-and-blue steps with their wonky leg.

Since my mother had gone, my father's evening meals had been an almost steady stream of toasted cheese and Cadbury's MiniRolls. He had his pipe, of course, but I wasn't sure if that constituted a meal or not. He would come in, weary and smelling of oil, and then fiddle around making my tea. Every meal was seasoned with guilt. His. Mine. 'You might at least do the plates.' He said it just once. From then on I washed up after every meal, standing on a stool to reach into the deep steel sink.

I was never sure if he expected me to make my own tea as well. There was nothing said. Just his disappointment hanging in the air like a deflated Yorkshire pudding. His favourite meal – tripe and onions – was a recipe known only to him. His way with the venous and quivering sheets of blubber was a mystery I had no intention of unravelling. Smoked haddock, his runner-up, held no such trepidation. It looked as easy as making a cup of tea.

If a boy saves his pocket money up for three days he can buy enough smoked haddock to feed a tired and hungry man. My savings weren't quite enough, I was a few pennies short, but the man in MacFisheries gave it to me anyway. 'It goes under the grill, doesn't it?' He came round to the front of the counter and put his arm around my shoulders. He told me to warm the grill first, to rub some butter on the fish and cook it for about ten minutes. Then he warned me not to get fancy with it. He led me out of the shop, still with his arm around me. 'He'll enjoy that, your dad.'

The Belling was one of those where you had to push in the knob as you put the flame to the gas. Easy when you aren't standing on the kitchen steps. Every click and spark makes your heart jump. You catch your breath and wait for the thing to go up in your face.

A fillet of smoked haddock takes about five minutes to cook under a domestic grill. You rub it with butter, shake over some black pepper, but no salt, and let the flames do the rest.

The haddock lies saffron yellow under the grill. The butter glistens on the fat flakes of fish. All is plump, sweet and juicy. It never looked like this when Mum cooked it.

Where is he? He is always here by six o'clock. It's now ten past. I cut two slices of bread and butter them. I have never known him eat more. Twenty past, half past. Where is he? The haddock is starting to curl up at the edges. The butter has set to a grainy slime, the fish is now dull with a milky residue that has trickled down and into the grill pan.

The fish is turning the colour of a pair of old stockings, the edges have buckled like a dead frog in the sun. My father's beloved smoked haddock is stone cold.

I hear the purr of my father's new Humber in the drive-way. His fish looks more like roadkill than supper. Perhaps I should just chuck it in the bin so he won't know. Then he wouldn't feel bad about being late. But the pong hanging in the kitchen will give me away. Damn Auntie Fanny, if she hadn't just died I could blame her.

My father comes in, his face a bit red, his hair newly cut. Aftershave. His piece of fish is now on the table, sandwiched between two glass plates. 'Where have you been? It's ruined.'

'No it's not, it's just how I like it.'

As he sits down and starts to eat I leave the room. It was supposed to be such a treat. Why be late tonight of all nights? He hasn't had smoked haddock for tea since Mummy died. Suddenly, the tears come from nowhere, they just well up. A great hot wave. Later, I walk into the kitchen to see if he has finished. He is sitting with his head in his hands. He's crying.

Birthday Cake

Today is my tenth birthday and no one has even mentioned a party yet. I guess they must be keeping it as a surprise. Last year's was one of the best days of my life. Mum said she couldn't cope with so many people any more so we held it at a big house on Coleway Road called the Pines. All the crocuses were out in the garden and because it was so close to Easter everyone gave me chocolate Easter eggs. I ended up with about thirty eggs, then Mum told me off because when the last person arrived I said 'Oh no, not another egg', and he looked really disappointed. She said something about me being ungrateful.

The Pines had someone there to organise the party. There was lots of running around and screaming. Much more than we had been allowed to do at other kids' parties. The best bit was the birthday cake, even though Mum didn't make it herself. She said it was too much for her. It was a great cake covered in Smarties and candles. We all took slices of it home, wrapped in paper serviettes, though mine stuck to the paper and all the colour came out of the Smarties. I felt bad afterwards because Paul Griffith's dad gave some of the boys a lift home and David Brooks was sick in the back of his car. I can't remember what happened to all the chocolate eggs.

I can't help feeling I should be doing more to help my dad, but I don't really know what. I have offered to cook my own tea but he says he doesn't want me messing with the Aga too much. He told me about an accident that happened a while ago when one of the Aga hotplate covers fell down and trapped the cleaner's hand on the hob. I have told him I will be very, very careful but he says that I shouldn't mess with it.

He bought sausages for the first time the other day but they were disgusting, like little pink rodents. They were the pinkest things I have ever seen. Mum used to buy big fat bangers with lots of black and green flecks in them. The ones Dad bought were on a polystyrene tray and didn't have any skin. He said he won't do them again. My dad hates shopping for food.

He leaves for work in the morning before I get up. I get washed and changed and walk to school with Warrel, who has been very sweet and kind to me since Mum died. I think his mum must have told him to be nice to me. Adults talk to you differently when your mum has died. A bit like you are stupid or made of glass. When your mum dies you remember everything people say. You put each word under a magnifying glass. It's like they are talking in capital letters. When your mum dies you notice little things more, like your senses are all cranked up a notch.

Apparently, I am not having a party this year. Dad says only girls have parties when they are ten.

Bed

My bedroom was small, barely wide enough for the bed, single wardrobe and chest of drawers, but at least I didn't have to share, like Adrian and John. My bed is the thing I remember most clearly about the house, the feathery softness of the pillows, the thick stitching on the Witney blankets, the missing tufts on the yellow candlewick bedspread. Yet I never felt truly safe there, the way I should have.

Going to bed had always been fraught. I wanted to stay up a bit later, a request always refused, kindly but emphatically by Mum; impatiently, and with eyes ablaze, by my father. When I was in trouble over something, usually for being cheeky or thoughtless, my father would send me to bed with the stern warning: 'I'll be up later to give you a damn good hiding.' I would snuggle down under the sheets, praying he would forget, twitching at every creak of the wooden floorboards in the hall, screwing up my eyes and burying my face at the sound of his footsteps on the stairs. I would lie there scrunched up in a ball under the sheets for an hour or more till I fell asleep. He would (almost) always forget.

After Mum died, going to bed was laced with a different horror. Night after night Dad would be out at one of his Masonic lodge meetings or working late at the factory. Sometimes I didn't even know where he was. With Adrian now at college and John living in London, I had to put myself to bed. Every floorboard at York House creaked; even with the lights on, the hall and staircase had a slightly malevolent air, the oak panelling making the house seem older and more sinister than it was. The fact that Auntie

Fanny had died in the bedroom next to mine less than six months before didn't exactly help. You wouldn't think it was possible to miss an old woman who couldn't hear a word you said and smelled of pee.

I would watch television till nine o'clock, then go and phone my Aunt Elvie. I would ask her, beg her, to hold on while I went upstairs and got ready for bed, then I would come running down and say goodnight. Having her listen while I got into my pyjamas made me feel safer. I could be back upstairs and snuggled into a ball under the sheets within seconds of her putting down the phone.

I never told my father I was scared to be alone at night. I don't know why. I just didn't.

Fairy Drops

Once in a while Dad would return home earlier than usual, a cancelled meeting perhaps, and take me off to the sweet shop.

The shelves were stacked with jars with stoppers so wide the shopkeeper could hardly get her hand round to screw them off. There were barley sugars for the elderly, mint humbugs for the patient and toffee eclairs for anyone without false teeth. My father bought buttered Brazils, their outsides gritty with sugar that would scratch on your teeth. Or pear drops that smelled of my mother's nail-varnish remover. I saw jelly babies coming over the counter, multicoloured liquorice torpedos and Clarnico Mint Creams. I would rarely see any of them again.

'What would you like? Go on, choose whatever you want.' I turned down everything except packets of Refreshers, Love Hearts and fairy drops. He always winced when I asked for fairy drops. 'Are you sure you wouldn't rather have some Brazil nut toffees?' he said, trying desperately to make a man of me.

You are probably supposed to like fairy drops for the nubbly spheres of multicoloured sugar that crown the little buttons of chocolate; but I liked them for the same reason I liked Cadbury's Flakes or Munchies, because no matter how fresh they were, I always thought they tasted ever so slightly stale.

Tinned Raspberries

A few weeks after my mother died we had tinned raspberries for tea. 'Can I take mine in the other room, Daddy?'

'If you're very careful. There's lots of juice.'

I hold the dish with both hands and wonder why he put quite so much juice in. But it is glorious juice. As garnet red as the stained-glass window behind the altar in St Stephen's, the heady smell wafts up like wine. I put the fruit carefully down on the little red-and-white footstool that Dad calls 'the poof' and drag it across the pale dove-grey carpet. Raspberries are the most gorgeous of the tinned fruit we have. Better than peaches, apricots, figs, even strawberries. And there is so much juice. My favourite.

I'm dragging the stool across the carpet and keeping a close eye on the juice level which is lapping at the edges of the dish. One of the front legs hits the rug in front of the fireplace and from now on everything is happening in slow motion. The stool judders and the dish bounces slowly off on to the carpet. It is upside down. I calmly walk into the kitchen and pick up the white dishcloth from behind the taps. 'You haven't?' yells my father and again, 'You haven't?'

I have. The juice is sinking into the carpet faster than I can mop it up. The stain, suddenly more like blood than juice, is getting wider, a full two feet across now. He storms in, his eyes are on fire. 'Give it here.' He grabs the dishcloth and dish out of my hand and slops the soggy fruit back where it came from. He dabs pointlessly at the juice on the carpet.

My father puts the dish down on the floor, in the middle of the stain. He yanks me back with the blue collar of my T-shirt. 'I ... told ... you ... to be ... careful.' A slap flashes across my ear with every word. 'I ... told ... you ... to ... be ... careful.' Harder now, he just keeps slapping and slapping. My ear, the side of the head, my neck. One catches my earlobe. I am in the corner by the door now, my back against the yellow wallpaper. I slide down to the floor. I put my hands up and over my head. He just keeps slapping. It is like he cannot stop. My ear is numb, my cheeks and head are stinging. My mouth is dry. Tears won't come. I want to go to the toilet.

Everything has stopped. The room is silent. He has gone. I stand up and pull my left sock up, which has ruckled down to my ankle. I walk through the hall and then through the kitchen. Past the garage I can see him in his greenhouse. He has got a pale pink begonia on the wooden slats and is pressing the soil tenderly down around the stem. He puts it back and picks up another, this time red. My father touches a bud with his thumb and forefinger, and then a flower, pulling the petals back softly, like he is calming a sparrow with a broken wing. His face is scarlet, puffed. There are tears running down it.

Scrambled Egg

'Just try it,' pleaded my father, holding out a plate of particularly yellow scrambled egg.'You won't taste the eggs, I promise.'

He had become cunning of late; a promised pancake had turned out to be an omelette, some slices of hard-boiled egg had been slipped into a salad sandwich and, in a moment of spectacular deceit, he had attempted to hide the yolk of a fried egg under a mound of baked beans.

I was having none of it. Every morsel of food was inspected both on the plate and again on the fork for signs of the dreaded *oeuf*. No lettuce leaf or bridge roll was left unchecked, no salad dressing went unsniffed, every sandwich was prised apart. The more wily he became, the more untrusting I learned to be. At one point I used to sit on the kitchen counter talking to him as he made supper, just to check that no new-laid wonder found its way on to my plate.

I promised I'd give it a go. He didn't leave the room. I sniffed the golden slop suspiciously. It did, sure enough, smell of cheese. The colour was deep and rich, like that of a crocus, and it had a clear moat of yellow fat round it, which looked the same as the fat which came out of one of his less successful attempts at cheese on toast. A timid forkful proved edible. A second went down easy enough and soon I had finished the lot. I am not sure who was happiest.

As the weeks went by my scrambled suppers became less manageable. By the fourth week, the egg had become detectable; by the sixth, the cheese was barely noticeable. But by this time my father had seen enough empty plates to know I could be trusted to eat up my supper without him peering over my shoulder. Sad, then, that I couldn't trust him not to gradually cut down on the cheese. Even sadder, then, that I started feeding it to the dog.

He would come home early all the time now. Only an hour or so after I got in from school he would appear and make me something to eat. Then he would leave the house in a whirlwind of aftershave and freshly ironed shirt, leaving me alone again, eating at the table. His cheeks had got more colour recently. His hair glistened with Brylcreem scooped from a red plastic pot and his face and neck scrubbed up as pink as a pork chop.

American Hard Gums

In the normal course of events my father and Mrs Potter never would have met. He didn't inhabit a world where women wore Crimplene. He had never come across a woman who did her housework with her hair in rollers. Come to think of it, he didn't even know any women who did their own housework, let alone other people's. They got to know one another through the raffles and whist drives they organised for a local disabled group. 'It nearly did my back in doing the waltz with Mr Guthrie,' Joan Potter announced one evening after a wheelchair dance in the function room of the Battle of Britain pub. 'I thought I was going to slip another bleedin' disc.'

She wore her hair in a tight perm like a First Division footballer. Her eyes were small and twinkling, like espresso coffee. Her mouth was as tight as a walnut and carried above it the faintest of moustaches. Yet she was strangely attractive and, dressed up for the evening, her hair done in softer curls, she was undeniably sexy. Especially to a man twenty years older and gagging for it.

It all started normally enough when my father's secretary, a pretty, moonfaced girl called Barbara, asked if he could help with a local charity with which her mother Joan Potter was involved. It took just a few weeks from buying the occasional raffle ticket to find him assisting in the fortnightly charity-raising events. (Say what you like about Joan Potter, she made a small fortune for the disabled.) Whenever he attended a beetle drive or coffee evening, Joan would be there. He passed the end of her street anyway, so why not drop her off afterwards. He knew the area well enough, though only because it was less than a mile from his factory. He didn't know anyone who actually lived in the maze of council estates and high-rise blocks. No one who might drink a pint of 'mild' at the Battle of Britain. No one who would care to spend an afternoon in the bingo hall. But, as he said, he passed the end of her street anyway.

Around the corner from Joan's house was a sweet shop that sold pear drops, Parkinson's Fruit Thins and things called American Hard Gums. As their name implied, they took some chewing. The colours were muted reds, greens and whites and reminded me of the lights we put on the tree at Christmas. My father adored them above all other sweets and would travel miles to get them. 'I haven't seen these for years,' he beamed one day, coming back to the car after dropping Mrs Potter off, clutching a small white paper bag of sweets. 'Try one, go on.'

The gritty sugar coating scratched across the enamel of my teeth. I chewed and I chewed. You could barely make a dent in them. My one and only Hard Gum lasted all the way home.

I started to notice just how often he would have a new white paper bag of gums on the dashboard of the Humber. The sweets became as much of a fixture of the car as the Shell map of Great Britain in the map pocket and the driving gloves in the glovebox. As much a fixture of the car as one Mrs Joan Potter.

Spinach

Stevie, my brother's new girlfriend, was everything in the kitchen my mother was not. When she came over for the evening she would always cook something for my brother. She cooked greens that shone emerald on the plate. Mother's greens had been the colours of an army surplus store. Stevie boiled ham hocks and grilled haddock; she flash-fried liver so it was rose pink in the middle and roasted potatoes so that they had crunchy outsides and fluffy white flesh within. She made steak and casseroles, jam tarts whose pastry crumbled tenderly when you picked them up, and velvety yellow custard in bowls so deep you could lose a small pet in it.

Stevie could get me to eat anything. Anything except eggs. It took her just one try to get me to like the spinach that I had sworn I would never let pass my lips. Once I had seen the way she sliced a lamb chop so as to get both pink meat and crispy fat on her fork at once, and how she ate it quickly, while the fat was still hot and wobbly and the meat juicy, it made me see the chop in a different light. From then on I couldn't have eaten it faster had it had Cadbury's embossed on it.

It is five past six on a Tuesday and my brother is due home. Stevie is sitting by the fire, brushing her hair, her legs curled under her. She is sorting letters into chronological order in her porcupine-quill writing case. She has kept every letter she has ever received, even the ones from her parents when she was at boarding school. Letters still in their envelopes, opened neatly with a letter-opener. I want to keep mine like this too, except no one has ever written me a letter.

She finishes brushing her hair and starts to do mine, which frankly could do with a cut. She runs the Mason and Pearson through my hair, making it curl at the ends. I think it makes me look like Brian Jones of the Stones.

Smoke

We only use a couple of pans now; the non-stick milk pan for warming up tinned tomatoes to go on toast, the old frying pan for cooking a bit of bacon on a Sunday morning. If you move any of the others tiny silverfish dart out from underneath. Last weekend there was a woodlouse in the roasting tin. Since Mum's gone the dishcloth always smells.

It seemed like we used to live on lamb chops, peas and boiled potatoes, but now I long to taste those chops again, Mum's boiled gammon too and the lumpy sauce she used to make with dried parsley. We haven't had fish – she used to fry it and serve it with Jif lemon – since last December. Cadbury's MiniRolls have replaced her pancakes and baked apples. I never thought it would be possible to get bored of Cadbury's MiniRolls.

Last night I came home to find the kitchen full of smoke. There was bacon under the grill and it had caught fire. I don't know where Dad was. We still ate it, charred and shattered with tinned tomatoes that he forgot to heat up. My father looks tired and as if he is on the point of saying something important, but never does. If it wasn't for the bread and butter this would be the worst meal I've had since Mum died. Not only that, my school pullover smells of grease and smoke.

Dad brought Mrs Potter to the house today. She smiled at me and said we both looked as if we needed fattening up.

Players No. 6 (Tipped)

I am not sure quite when Mrs Potter started as our cleaner. I only know that she did. Every day except Wednesdays I would come home at lunchtime to the warm dough smell of fresh ironing and a cooked meal. There was a coldness to Mrs Potter, a distance, as if she didn't quite approve of me, but her cooking was a dream come true. Bits of steak with grilled tomatoes and home-made chips as long as my fingers; pork chops with the kidney left in and apple rings done in the frying pan; slices of gammon with pineapple rings and, once, a cherry like the one in Marguerite Patten's book.

She would sit there tight-lipped while I ate. Never at the table, always on a chair against the wall, a Players No. 6 in her hand. When she heard my father's car pull up outside, she would squeeze the lighted tip of her cigarette between her thumb and finger and put it in her apron pocket, then fan the air and pull her skirt straight.

If I dawdled at the table after lunch, for example, when there was a dreaded PE lesson or when I knew I was going to get bullied in the playground, he would say, 'Go along now, go and play.' Mrs Potter seemed shy in my presence, cool and formal. She spoke quietly and reluctantly, yet she and my father never looked away from each other. What came out of their mouths, stiff, crisp, rather correct, was very different from what their eyes were saying. It was as if they had known each for years and had a separate, private language. That language that parents mistakenly, patronisingly think their children cannot comprehend. A language so loud, so painful, so icily clear that it is as if they were plunging a kitchen knife deep into your chest.

Tinned Beans and Sausage

My father never made it home to lunch on Wednesdays. It was also Mrs P.'s day off. My lunch was always left in the oven; a clear glass dish beaded with condensation, the contents invariably bean and sausage casserole.

This was not a rustic earthware pot of haricot beans and garlic-laced *saucisse*, but an upturned tin of baked beans with chipolata sausages in them, left to warm up and then congeal in the slow oven of the Aga. It was a sad sight to come home to. Three thin skinless bangers in a mess of brown beans, a thin skin lying over the top like a shroud. Made with love it could have looked like a Robert Freson photograph, a warming peasant lunch in a much loved and battered casserole handed down through the family. Instead, it looked like an unflushed lavatory.

Yet there was something I looked forward to about this meal. Opening the leaden door of the Aga, the scary blast from the hot oven, lifting out the dish by the tiny glass handles you could barely feel through thick oven gloves. It was as near as I had got to cooking since the haddock episode.

One day I came home to an empty oven. My father had forgotten. The dog, who hated being left alone, had peed on the kitchen floor. I found an opened packet of Ritz crackers, sat and ate them, salty tears streaming down my face. It wasn't that I even liked the tinned beans and sausages. I just liked the idea that someone had remembered to leave me something to eat.

Banana Custard

Quite the best thing about my brother's new girlfriend was her ability to make a decent banana custard. In fact, it was better than decent, it was sublime: warm, sweet, creamy, soothing and with just the right ratio of Bird's custard to bananas. Stevie knew not only to make the sauce thick enough to hold the bananas in suspension, but how thin to slice the fruit. Too thick and the bananas failed to flavour the custard properly, too thin and they collapsed into the sauce. She always got it right.

None of us ever quite knew when Adrian was due home. Sometimes it would be on the dot of six, other times it would be nearer eight o'clock. The dessert was always better for an hour on the back of the Aga, a time in which the fruit would steep and slowly flavour the creamy yellow depths. Stevie would start boiling the milk and mixing the custard powder and granulated sugar at about six o'clock. She would pour the foaming milk on to the dry mix and stir slowly, the sauce becoming heavier by the second. She would slice the bananas over the custard, letting each piece drop down and sink into the depths of the dish so they had no time to brown. Then she would cover the bowl with tinfoil and lift it over the hotplate to the back of the Aga. There it would stay until my brother came home.

It is almost impossible to steal a spoonful of custard without leaving a trail of clues behind. Even if a skin hasn't formed, the tell-tale signs of theft are there for all to see. The broken calm of the yellow surface; the paler yellow showing through the deeper yellow of the skin; the all-too-careful repair. Over the months before they married I perfected my dishonesty, digging into my brother's dessert time and again while Stevie had a bath.

It was only when Adrian was extraordinarily late one night and I had returned several times to dip in that I got caught. I hadn't noiced that I had eaten all but one slice of banana. 'If you'd eaten them all he would never have noticed,' said Stevie later, 'he would have assumed I'd just made custard.'

Strawberries and Cream

During the winter months the Masonic ladies' night became an almost weekly occurrence. Neither sleet nor storm would keep my father, crisp and scrubbed in his white tux and Old Spice, from attending. His small, recently bereaved son became a regular fixture at the various Masonic lodges, the sinister male-only halls with their blacked-out windows that were hastily transformed into venues suitable for female visitors. As regular as the extravagant floral displays that for one night each year were used to hide the urinals in the temporary women's lavatories.

I had no idea how honoured I was to be allowed to attend each lodge's annual parade of wives in their ballgowns. Mrs Wood in claret velveteen, Eunice Everard in bottle-green taffeta, and Minnie Clarke in a suitably plain blue satin number she'd obviously knocked up specially for the occasion. I was unaware of the disapproval among the more conservative members who found a little boy's attendance at such an occasion inappropriate. I should have spotted it. After all, these were the sort of men who thought a bunch of pale yellow carnations and a spray of asparagus fern were enough to disguise a six-foot porcelain trough and its hearty whiff of urine.

One early-spring chicken dinner was followed by strawberries and cream. The whipped cream piled high on the mounds of blatantly unripe strawberries found few takers on our table. 'Hummmph. I knew they wouldn't be ripe,' chimed Eunice Everard, her face as sour as the berries that had promised so much on the copperplate menu. Dish after dish was passed down to the greedy little boy who could barely contain his excitement at such a feast. Soon, dishes of green-shouldered fruit were being passed over heads and across rows. 'I bet you can't eat them all,' said some wag.

Coffee was served and everyone was getting up to leave the room and the little boy was still tucking in. It wasn't the berries I was relishing. It was the gritty sugar and billowing cream with which the chef had smothered every bowl bar the one reserved for Mr Wood the diabetic.

The waiters cleared the white cloths and the coffee cups. The bare wooden trestles they had been hiding were stacked in a corner, the room swept of sugar wrappers, ready for the arrival of the band and the dancing ladies. I was left in the middle, a private island of gluttony, stuffing away green strawberries like my life depended on it.

You can get an awful lot of vomit in a wash-hand basin. Even so, once the deep white sink was full, and the two closets occupied, there was nowhere to turn but the urinal.

We did the long drive home, me half asleep in the back of the Humber. The heavy scent of vomit, strawberries and disgust filling the car. My father broke the silence just once. 'You might have had the intelligence to pull the sink plug out first. Just think of the poor cleaner who's got to dip their hand in that lot.'

The Dead Dog

'Oh, I forgot to tell you, Mrs Potter phoned and said she can't find her dog.'

My father glares at me. 'When, when did she phone?' I admit it was earlier that morning and I am sorry that I have forgotten to tell him. 'You stupid, stupid little fool,' he says, pacing to and fro across the kitchen floor. Then he gets in the car and drives off.

Later, he gives me a lecture about not forgetting to pass on important messages and tells me how he had found her dog dead, a group of men standing round it in the doorway of the pub wondering who it belonged to. How it had been hit by a car and how he had to go and break the news to her. Then he tells me it might not have happened if I had told him earlier. I feel thoroughly wretched about it but I can't see why he's making such a big deal of it. She's only the cleaner.

Bourbon Biscuits

Mrs Potter lived to clean. She said that dirt got on her 'nerves'. Friends, relatives, neighbours were measured by how often they polished their brass, swept their front step and, above all, by how well they cleaned their windows. No sink went unscrubbed, no table unpolished, no shirt unironed. Even doused in Topaz, the perfume she bought from her daughter's Avon catalogue, there was a faint undernote of Pledge to her.

Mrs P. enjoyed cleaning the way some people enjoy gardening or do-it-yourselfery. What she was going to clean next was the topic of her every conversation. Cigarette in one hand, melamine mug of Maxwell House in the other, she would list everything she had scrubbed, dusted, tidied or polished that day and then follow it with a list of everything she planned to scrub, dust, tidy or polish tomorrow. She once spent half a day removing the false patina from a much-loved wooden rococo mirror frame in the sitting room. 'Oh dear,' said my father, seeing the packet of spent Brillo pads and explaining that it was supposed to be like that. 'Well, it looked filthy to me.'

Filthy was one of Mrs Potter's favourite words. Like the 'revolting' she used to describe the way I ate biscuits such as Bourbons or custard creams. She pronounced it with a short 'o'. As in revolver. I was hardly the only child to nibble the top biscuit from a Bourbon cream, then lick off the chocolate filling with long, slow strokes as if it were an ice cream. To me the biscuit was boring, just packaging really; the filling, however, was to be savoured, allowed to melt slowly on the tongue. Mrs Do-it-and-dust-it regarded the habit as 'disgusting', but only because it invariably left one with sticky fingers, which could, if a ten-year-old boy was so inclined, be used to sabotage her shining woodwork.

Garibaldis

I have no idea why I have been spending so much time with Mrs Potter's family. Last week I went to her daughter's birthday party, and on Saturday I made fairy cakes from Viota cake mix with her middle daughter (she let me spoon the icing on top and arrange the jelly diamonds and hundreds and thousands). Yesterday, I sat at the back of her youngest daughter's hairdressing business. At least two of Mrs Potter's daughters have successful hairdressing salons, no wonder her hair always looks like it's just been 'done'. Today I'm in the little room behind the net-curtained salon reading *Rupert* annuals and trying not to breathe in the hydrogen peroxide that wafts in from the shop. It smells like stinkbombs. I don't know where Dad and Mrs Potter are. And I have absolutely no idea why I am here instead of playing with my friends. If it wasn't for the tin of biscuits on the table I would demand to go home. And to be honest, there are only three Garibaldis and a pink wafer left now.

The Lion, the Witch and the Wardrobe

I'm waiting patiently for Warrel to finish his tea. Minnie prises the lid off a tin of Tea Time Assorted and offers it to him. There must be fifty biscuits stacked in neat red cellophane compartments and there is a brief moment when I think she might point the tin at me but she doesn't. So I sit and watch Warrel munching his way through two Jammie Dodgers, a ginger nut and a milk chocolate wafer. Just as he is taking a swig of his Cremola Foam (and I am secretly hoping he is going to choke) Minnie asks me if Mum had a sewing machine and, if in fact she had, would my dad like to sell it. I honestly don't know so tell her that I will ask him.

Instead, I ask Mrs Potter who goes off like a rocket, accusing Minnie Blubb of being heartless to ask such a question so soon after Mum's death. 'She's not getting her hands on anything,' bites a spectacularly animated Mrs P., like Minnie was asking for her wedding ring. For the life of me I cannot quite see what Dad would want with Mum's sewing machine or why the cleaner is getting so het up about it. It's not like it's hers or anything. Come to think of it, I'm not sure Mum even had one.

Two or three days later I come home to find Mrs Potter wearing one of Mum's aprons. There is no reason on earth why she shouldn't, but it makes me feel uncomfortable. Especially since her outburst the other day.

It is four-thirty and I've just come home from school. I walk upstairs and see Dad's bedroom door open. Last time I tried to open the door, the morning Mum died, it banged against an oxygen tank that someone had put in the way. I open her wardrobe, and let its four hinged doors slowly unfold.

The wardrobe smells of Mum. Not her perfume or her lipstick, not her clothes or her Ventolin. Just her. I run my hands down the tight curls of her astrakhan coat, her summer dress with its white pearl buttons and blousy red poppies, her shimmery ballgown. I open the deep drawers in her dressing table and sniff her cardigans, her long evening gloves, her hankies. I open Mum's jewellery box and pull out her pearl necklace, her cameo brooch and another gold one in the shape of a feather. The one she always wore with her mushroom twinset. Even the quilted lining of the box smells of her.

Halfway along the rail in the wardrobe is her crinkly white petticoat, the one she wore under her ballgown when she and Dad went out for the evening. When he used to wear his black suit with the satin collar and his blue silk cummerbund. When they used to come back so late. I slide the petticoat straps off the wooden hanger that says Ventnor Hotel, Isle of Wight, and run my fingers over the huge swirls of black stitching. It feels like fuzzy felt. I lower it to the floor and step into it then pull the straps up and over my shoulders. The frills at the bottom touch the floor and rustle and swish like they are made of crêpe paper. I take out her favourite shoes, the ones we walked Wolverhampton for, the ones the colour of a foal. I slip my feet into them but they are too big. I can barely keep them on my feet. I hold Mum's pearls around my neck but I don't think she ever wore them with this petticoat.

One by one I touch everything in her wardrobe, the camel coat, the fawn jersey dress, the black woollen suit that always made her look cross, holding them against my face. In the mirror I look so small in Mum's stuff, and my feet slide around in her shoes when I walk across the room.

I take off her shoes, her white petticoat and put everything back, then I close the wardrobe door and creep back downstairs.

Salade Tiède

On the days Mrs Potter was cleaning at York House she would leave her husband's lunch between two plates, leaving him only to put it over a pan of water on the stove. Irish stew, chops and peas, ham and parsley sauce were all heated up this way. The method worked well enough, at least it did for a man who liked his meat well done.

Mrs Potter was truly the cleaner from heaven. For the first time since Mrs Muggeridge was fired, every surface in the house sparkled. The red tiled floors in the porch and downstairs loo shone with Cardinal polish, every table and chair was given a weekly treatment with lavender wax as well as a daily one with Pledge. She cleaned places that had never seen a brush or cloth before; the bit between the Aga and the dog basket, the back of the gramophone, the vents of the venetian blinds. A dust bunny didn't stand a cat in hell's chance.

As the weeks wore on she started complaining that it was all too much for her. 'This house is too big for one person, I can't do everything the way I want it. Could I bring my sister Ethel in to help?' The way she wanted it was far cleaner than any house deserved to be. Drop a sweet wrapper in the waste-paper basket and it was emptied before you could say humbug. Make a skidmark on the lavatory pan and it was brushed and flushed quicker than you could say shit.

Ethel wore black and smelled of mothballs. A little shrew of a woman, she never spoke when my father was around, not a word. It wasn't that she was intimidated by him, just completely overawed by the wealthy man for whom she worked and for whom her sister quite obviously had 'feelings'.

'He's like a film star,' Ethel once said to her sister.

'It's best that she comes too,' Mrs P. told my father, 'then if "he" says anything I can tell him to ask Ethel. She'll tell him there's nothing going on.' I am not sure my father could imagine Ethel saying anything to anyone. I am not sure he believed she could even speak.

Mrs P. rarely talked about her husband, though I knew he existed. I came home to lunch one day to find the two sisters talking about him. Or at least Joan was talking. I stood outside the kitchen door and listened to her telling Ethel how much she hated going back home to him and how she had, in hushed, ominous tones, other plans. 'And you'll never believe what the stupid old bugger did yesterday,' she cackled. 'He put his dinner on the cooker without looking to see what it was.' She could barely speak for laughing, 'He took the plate off and found he'd steamed himself a nice ham salad.'

The Day She Darned Dad's Socks

Suddenly everything seemed to be about Mrs Potter. 'Tidy your room up, will you?' says Dad and then adds, 'Mrs Potter will be here and she's got too much to do as it is.' Before she turned up on a Monday morning I had to put all my toys away in their wooden chest, straighten my books on their shelves and pick up the clothes that I threw on the floor when I got ready for my bath. Until that point I had never tidied up my room, or any room for that matter. I thought that's what we had a cleaner for. But this was different. It was like the queen was coming.

Dad always wore a tie to work, even when he used to come back red-faced and smelling of oil. Now, though, he came back to lunch clean and smelling of Old Spice. We had always eaten our lunches together, when he would ask me about school and what I was up to. But he seemed impatient with me now and kept saying things like 'Hadn't you better get off now, won't you be late back to school?'

Then Dad started coming late for his lunch, so he got home only five minutes or so before I had to leave. He said it was because someone at work wanted to have their lunch early, but I couldn't help thinking it was because he wanted to be with Mrs Potter more than he wanted to be with me.

Mrs Potter had started to be nice to me, often patting

the back of my head and calling me 'lad'. Her smiles were tight and shallow, but she would always bring the conversation round to me when my father was there. 'He's growing up so quickly now, isn't he?' and 'He ate all his peas today.' It was odd the way she talked about me as if I was invisible. One day in April, just before my birthday, I came home at four-thirty to find she was still there, sitting on the floor in the sitting room, her back up against Auntie Fanny's old chair. Even though we'd had it recovered it still smelled of pee. She was darning Dad's socks. Mrs Potter had the contents of my dad's sock drawer spread out on the carpet, every one neatly matched; those she had darned laid out smugly, the others folded into a ball. She must have sewn up the holes in at least twenty pairs.

I made a cheeky comment about it probably being cheaper for Dad to buy new socks than pay her to repair them. 'We don't all do things for money, young man,' she snapped. 'As it happens, I'm doing this just because I want to, I won't be getting paid for it. It's not easy for your dad now, you know. There's no one to do these things for him any more.' She licked the end of a piece of cotton, then screwed up her eyes as she tried to thread the end of it into the eye of the needle. 'I don't like the idea of him walking around with holes in his socks.'

I went up to my room, closed the door and put on 'Paint it Black' as loud as I dared. What had it got to do with her if my dad had holes in his socks?

Bluebird Milk Chocolate Toffees

'Get ready, we're going for a ride in the car,' Dad said one Saturday morning in early summer. He said it in that way he had of making something sound quite ordinary when it was obvious it was going to be anything but.

An hour later we were following the signs for Worcester. Dad wasn't saying much, which meant there was definitely something brewing. 'Are we going to see Auntie Betty?' I asked hopefully, loving every second of that particular aunt's company, especially when she said things like bugger and shit and my father looked at his shoes in embarrassment.

'Well, yes and no. Do you remember saying how much you would like to live at Betty's house?'

I did, but what I had actually meant was that I wanted to live with Auntie Betty rather than move to Clayford, her whitewashed eighteenth-century cottage in Knightwick.

'Well, Auntie Betty has decided the house is too big for her and has moved to Hereford and so we've bought Clayford. I wanted it to be a surprise.'

He waxed on about the bluebell woods, the orchard at the top of the garden, the possibility of my having a rabbit. It wasn't until he mentioned that it had been no problem getting me into the local school that I realised Clayford was to be more than a weekend cottage. That isolated, bitterly cold little house was to be our new home.

After a long silence (I didn't know what to say) I asked my first and last question. 'Will my friends be able to come and stay?'

He reached over and took a new packet of chocolate toffee eclairs out of the glovebox. 'Why don't you open these up. I know they are your favourites.' Wrong again. My favourites were Bluebird Milk Chocolate Toffees. I liked sucking the white-freckled chocolate, which somehow always seemed slightly stale to me, from the toffees, slowly, deliberately, while covering my tongue and teeth with the smooth, fatty chocolate. Chocolate eclairs worked the other way round, so you had to suck the toffee to get the chocolate.

We must have been within a mile or two of Clayford when he finally broke the heavy, on-the-edge-of-tears silence. 'You like Joan, don't you?'

I didn't answer.

'Doesn't she remind you of Mummy?'

We turned into the long driveway, the fat tyres crunching slowly on the gravel, tumbling yellow roses rubbing against the driver's side of the car. Clayford sat at the top of a one-in-six hill overlooking most of Worcestershire. Two vast lawns, split by a tall yew hedge, sloped lazily down to the drive and to the woods, our woods, beyond. Even freshly painted for its recent sale, the house bore a faintly sad expression, as if it knew it faced the wrong way. Instead of looking out at the rolling fields, hamlets and streams and the Malvern Hills beyond, its six front windows stared at the garage, albeit a rather quaint one, covered with honeysuckle and clematis montana. Only the tiny scullery overlooked 'the view'. This was a house probably better to visit than to live in. Auntie Betty had told us that in summer, cars would continually slow up or even stop, their passengers getting out to admire the clipped lawns, the pillows of mauve aubrietia and billowing honeysuckle, and above all 'the view'. 'Imagine living here,' they would say, as if having no neighbours, no friends and a septic tank was a good thing.

The house, a good hundred yards away from the drive, stood basking in the sun. It looked different, for once its ragged lawns clipped like those of a bowling green, which had the effect of making the cascading roses and marguerites look curiously out of place, like drunken guests lying around after a party. Now the edges were crisp, sharp as razors. Auntie Betty's windows had always been a bit grubby. We used to joke about them and how she once said she hated cleaning them and did the job 'once a year whether the buggers needed it or not'. But today they shone like jet in the sunshine. Six deep, black pools glistening like army boots.

Victoria Sandwich

She was sitting there in one of the garden chairs, tight lips, tight perm, twenty Embassy and a cigarette lighter in her lap. 'Say hello to your Auntie Joan,' my father said quietly, enunciating her new name slowly and firmly.

'You can call me Auntie Joanie if you want to,' said Mrs Potter. I walked straight past her and round to the kitchen door. 'I told you,' she snapped at my father.

'Just give him time, he'll be all right,' said Dad.

There was a cake on the spotless kitchen table. A home-made cake, with a thin line of raspberry jam in the middle, the top dusted with caster sugar. A perfect cake, three inches high and as light as a feather, the criss-cross of the wire cooling rack etched into its soft, golden top. The kitchen smelled of baking and Dreft. Two pairs of my underpants and my school pullover hung on a wooden airer with some tea towels still warm from the iron. Mrs Potter rushed in behind me.

'Come on, I'll put the kettle on. Why don't we make some toast?'

Ham

The mobile shop came on Thursdays. Cool and dark inside, it smelled of boiled ham and links of pork sausage. During the school holidays I would stand on the fold-down step with Auntie Joan watching while the grocer cut thin slices of ham from the bone. No wibbly-wobbly jelly here. Just thin, cool, pink ham, soft as a baby's tummy. We bought tomatoes that smelled warm and herbal; soft-leaved lettuces

144

and packets of salty butter; Saxa salt and Lion brand ground black pepper in little drums; bottles of Heinz Salad Cream, tinned peaches and Princes tinned crabmeat.

In winter he would come later, just as I got home from school, and I would help bring in bags of sugar and flour, tins of soup, trifle sponges and Ambrosia Creamed Rice, flat boxes of Dairylea triangles, hunks of Cheddar with the muslin on, Cornish wafers, crumpets, Oxo cubes, Pickering's Cherry Pie Filling and bottles of Tree Top orange drink.

The baker arrived on Tuesdays and Fridays and we bought a bloomer or a cottage loaf. He sometimes had six-packs of fairy cakes with coloured buttercream, hundreds and thousands and a blob of vivid red jam on top. I regularly ate three of the six. We kept the ham till Saturday when we had sandwiches with the soft, fresh bread and freshly cut cress on the lawn.

Every meal was now a proper meal. Meat, potatoes and vegetables and usually, but not always, a pudding. In summer we had tinned salmon and cucumber salad, new potatoes and trifle. In winter Joan would get a fug up in the kitchen, boiling a piece of ham and making thick parsley sauce, spinach and mashed potatoes. Then there would be rice pudding or apple pie and custard. Every now and again we would have a mixed grill on oval plates. A little piece of steak, a kidney opened up like a butterfly, a lobe of lamb's liver, tomatoes, black pudding and sometimes a sausage or a chop. Then there were mushrooms, big flat ones the size of a tea saucer, and of course chips. She would do a stew now and again, thickened with pearl barley and served with mashed swede or parsnips. I liked the broth that surrounded it, and the bland, dead flavours. 'I'd do it more often if the smell didn't carry through the house like it does,' she would say, beaded lines of condensation running down every window.

Breakfast held no fears. The egg incidents seemed from another world. There would be hot toast, salty butter and Rose's lime marmalade. My father had Robertson's orange instead and let me send off the labels for golly badges. He only told me off once, when I left a bit of butter in the marmalade jar. Even then he didn't really seem to mind. He let me climb on his lap more now.

One day Joan showed me how to make a Victoria sandwich, which she always called sponge. 'The reason it rises so well is because I use Blue Band Soft margarine,' she confided as I lined the sponge tins. She let me beat the sugar and marg with the egg beater till it came up in a white fluff; we added large eggs from the farm, one at a time, and then self-raising flour. Joan let me dollop the cake mixture into the buttered tins, and smooth the tops level with the back of a spoon. They didn't rise quite as much that time, but they tasted the same. We swapped the raspberry jam for apricot, which everyone preferred. 'You'll be able to make it yourself next time,' Dad said as he picked up a slice the size of a small island, the caster sugar falling off on to his waistcoat. I would have too, but from then on the cakes were always baked and ready when I came home from school. Sitting there in the middle layer of the new stack of see-through cake tins, just below the jam tarts and above her perfect apple pie.

Boiled Ham and Parsley Sauce

There are smells that define a home. Ours smelled of boiled gammon, parsley sauce and what Joan, in a futile attempt to be middle class, called 'creamed' potatoes.

A smell which, encountered at another time, another place, would bring back every swirl of sitting-room carpet, every piece of knotty-pine kitchen unit, each and every melamine cup and saucer; the creak of the green Parker-Knoll rocking chair and the click of Joan's knitting needles (I thought I'd do you an Aran sweater for your Christmas box); the scent of Dad's red and salmon begonias in the greenhouse; the smell of my Matey bubblebath, her Camay soap and his Signal toothpaste. It would bring back Fluff Freeman and his Top Twenty countdown, the stuttering telex printing out the football scores on *Grandstand*, 'Jumpin' Jack Flash' and the Epilogue.

That smell would also bring back the long silences when Joan and I were alone in a room; the long, long summer holidays with no one to play with; doing my homework in the freezing dining room just so I could listen to *Sgt Pepper*; but most clearly, of the wet-eyed glare my father would shoot at me when I said anything that could be taken, even remotely, as a slight against Joan.

The gammon came not from the mobile shop but from the butcher at the bottom of the hill. The queues – they were open just three days a week – were almost a social event. You caught up on the local gossip while waiting for your 'nice bit of silverside'. The meat, particularly the beef, was legendary, with customers driving from as far as Bromyard for their Sunday joint. It was a bloody butcher's shop, with red splashes up the creamy-yellow flyblown walls, bits of meat on the floor and more flies than you could flick a swat at. When the butcher lifted a piece of sirloin up from his block the air would turn black with bluebottles. Yet it stopped no one. 'There's no meat like it for miles,' they said. 'I think it's revolting,' sniffed Joan the first time, as she closed the car door, her arms folded tight across her chest. 'He should be closed down.' Yet my father insisted there was nothing to compare and he was right.

When we first moved to Clayford the parsley for the sauce came from a jar in the larder, one of the wooden-topped bottles in the spice rack Mum had bought a good seven years before. The cloves were opened only when anyone had toothache, the mixed-spice jar was occupied by allspice berries (not, of course, that anyone actually knew), and the sun had parched the dried chives to the colour of hay, which is no doubt exactly what they tasted of. Even now visitors would marvel at the dark wooden rack with its black-and-gold labels. I think we were all too embarrassed to ask what you were supposed to do with mace.

Once Dad started to grow rows of parsley plants ('I could never get the buggers to germinate till Percy Thrower told us to pour boiling water on the seeds') the Tuesday ham became something of a joy, its sauce suddenly lush and vivid. Despite the calm blip-blop of the ham simmering in its deep pan of water, the last few minutes were always ones of unsuppressed panic. Joan would break out into a sweat beating the butter and hot milk into the potatoes, the accompanying spinach had to go on at the last minute, and the windows would be all fugged up from the ham. The meat had to be lifted from the steaming water and carved, the spinach drained and the sauce warmed up in a non-stick saucepan. Offers of help were always on the tip of my tongue but never actually came out. Instead, I spent five minutes putting the place mats on the table and another five straightening the cutlery. Then I would stand behind the door pretending to do something important. Joan would put the last plate of pink, white and green on the table, sigh audibly and finally take off her apron and throw it over the draining board. I never knew what to say.

Mushing the sauce into the creamy clouds of potato was as much a treat as the ham itself. Nothing I ate all week came close to that first forkful of pink ham with its little ear of white fat and its green-flecked, creamy slick of potato and sauce.

Green Beans

Clayford worked neither as a house nor a home. To see 'the view' you had to go into the scullery or the dining room, which was only used at Christmas and was kept permanently just above freezing. My father said this was to make the Christmas cactus flower on time.

The layout was absurd and embarrassing. I had to walk through my father's bedroom to get to mine, an awkward low-ceilinged room with a view of the road on one side. He could hear every breath I took, every page I turned, every rustle of my sheets. Masturbating without him hearing became an art in itself. The bathroom sat directly above the kitchen. I lost count of how many times we sat around the dinner table in silence, listening to my father and his spectacular flatulence in the room above. I smirked at every fart. 'Giggle and I'll send you up to bed,' Joan would threaten as I glared down intently at my liver and mash.

Brilliant-white Snowcem partly hid the fact that the house was a mishmash of seventeenth-century cottage and 1920s new money. Joan was never happier than when she had spent the day with the paint bucket, hiding the speckles of black mould that showed through when the damp weather came. 'People might think it's dirt.' And she did win the moss war, devilling out every bit of fluffy green lichen from the garden walls with the handle of an old spoon. I suspect my father rather liked his moss. 'It gets on my nerves,' she would say. I seem to remember almost everything getting on her nerves.

Friday morning was when she polished the copper and brass. The reproduction copper warming pan that hung behind the fireplace, the horseshoes that framed the grate and the brass fire-stand with its shovel, coal tongues and hearth brush that we were forbidden to use. Most prized were the crocodile nutcrackers that wouldn't crack a Malteser let alone a Brazil nut. To this day I won't have a copper pan in the house. I can still see her sitting there in her lemon nylon housecoat, rubbing away at her bloody brass crocodile.

My father had taken to growing his own food. There had always been the fruit trees, the green and golden gages, the Victoria and Drooper plums that were so bent they had to be held up with an uneven pile of bricks, and the apple trees that never let us down, but he started growing vegetables too, everything from onions to tobacco, broad beans to sweetcorn. He was good at it too, showering us with more fruit and vegetables than we knew what to do with. We took to salting beans. First, you slice the beans with a tiny, sharp knife – which Joan could do almost as fast as she could count the notes in a wage packet – then you layered them in an old, square-shouldered sweetie jar with salt. As the winter wore on, the salt coroded the lid, so badly that rivulets of poisonous black juice would run down into the snowy white beans. 'Don't be so daft,' she would snap as I turned my nose up at the stained vegetables, 'they just need a good rinse.'

'Go and Play'

New School. The scariest words in a child's world. Scarier still when your rise to secondary school coincides with a move across country, at one swoop reducing the chances of knowing at least one kid from your junior school to zero.

We had driven past the Chantry at least a dozen times since we moved to Knightwick. Half timbered, half hidden by trees, ancient and unthreatening. As the summer holidays wore on I almost looked forward to going to a school a tenth of the size of Woodfield, with creaking floorboards and vast chimneys. It would be like being in a Malcolm Saville book. The morning I left for the school bus, neat in my new black blazer, short trousers and squeaky new shoes, I was more excited than scared. School looked a distinctly better option than staying at home.

It wasn't. The Chantry we had admired was now the local junior school, the main school had moved to fields across the road; a newly built 1960s glass and brick affair, where the classrooms were painted 'experimental' dark blues and greens and the corridors had squeaky chequered vinyl floors. Squeaky new floors for squeaky new shoes. In modern terms it was intimate, a mere three hundred pupils, with a swimming pool, vegetable garden and playing fields that went to the horizon. But when you are expecting your school bus to turn left and it turns right it also turns your world upside down.

At the Chantry you either lived on a farm or your parents worked on one. If not, then there was one next door. At weekends you mucked out stables, fed the lambs or went pheasant-beating, depending on the time of year. During the holidays you helped get in the strawberries, beans, potatoes or hops. Even I got a job picking blackcurrants, till Dad found out I was working with gypsies and put a stop to it. The best lesson was rural science with Charles Ritson, in a room that smelled of potting compost. The worst was woodwork with the vile Mr Oakley, who slapped your fingers with a metal ruler if your plane went in a wonky line. To this day my stomach flips over if I smell newly planed wood.

School friends were exactly that. Once you got on the bus home you never saw them till next morning. Dad and Joan loved the peace and quiet, the fact that you had to drive three miles to get the *Telegraph* or four for a loaf of bread. It didn't seem to bother them that come the summer holidays I saw no one but them for an entire six weeks. And it wasn't like they wanted me there. 'Go and play', 'Go and walk in the woods', 'Go and clean your rabbit out',

'Go and find something to do'. What they really meant was 'Just GO'.

Knightwick wasn't much of a village: a post office with lavender at the gate, an old pub with beams and horse brasses, and a quaint church, but that was it really. If you crossed the river by the little bridge, you came to the butcher's shop in a pretty red-brick cottage with roses around its door and the doctor's house whose striped lawns sloped down to the river. Each summer there was a fête in the field – the usual jars of bramble jelly and buttercream-filled sponge cakes, plants in pots and goldfish in bowls. If you wanted more of a spectacle you could drive to the Madresfield Show, which we did. The cottages that speckled the steep hill up to Clayford had hollyhocks in the garden and were charming enough, but hardly what you would call 'chocolate box'. The only stir in six long summers was when a group of hippies took up residence in a cottage hidden in the woods, but I was forbidden from going up there. 'You never know what you might get mixed up in,' said my father. Someone from the village said they danced around in the garden, naked.

Lemon Meringue Pie

Joan's lemon meringue pie was one of the most glorious things I had ever put in my mouth: warm, painfully sharp lemon filling, the most airy pastry imaginable (she used cold lard in place of some of the butter) and a billowing hat of thick, teeth-judderingly sweet meringue. She squeezed the juice of five lemons into the filling, enough to make you close one eye and shudder. The pie was always served warm, so the filling oozed out like a ripe Vacherin.

Joan had picked up the recipe from her youngest daughter Mary. I wanted so much to make it, to have a go, but she kept the method close to her chest. She always seemed to make the vast marshmallowy pie when I wasn't around. 'You should be getting on with your homework' was all the answer I got when I asked if I could help. When I once asked sweetly for the recipe, she told me she couldn't remember. 'It just comes into my head once I get started' was all she would say.

I would invent reasons to walk through the kitchen as the secret pie was being made, picking up a single detail each time, counting egg shells or lemon skins in the bin while she was watching *The Persuaders*. I amassed the recipe bit by bit as I sneaked through the kitchen on some trumped-up errand for my father. I spotted the five egg yolks and the lemon juice, the three tablespoons of cornflour and the five of sugar, and the three ounces of butter in the filling. I caught the blind-baking of the pastry case and even clocked the oven temperature (375°F) and the all-important point at which she would catch the whipped egg whites before folding in the sugar. But I never once got the chance to make it.

There were other secrets too. The way she cooked chips twice to get them fluffy and crisp. The intimate details of treacle tart or the essentials of decorating a melon wedge with a slice of orange and a maraschino cherry. But there was plenty I was encouraged to help with: washing up, drying the dishes, ironing tea towels, cleaning out the guinea pig's cage, turning the compost, getting the washing in, making tea, taking the bin out, bringing in the logs. 'If you were any sort of a lad at all, you'd go and help your father chopping the logs rather than folding tea towels.'

Salad Cream, Mushroom Ketchup and Other Delights

Tomato ketchup has never set foot over our threshold, unlike Burgess's Mushroom Ketchup with which Dad is besotted, especially on bacon and, of course, on his grilled mushrooms. He says it makes them more mushroomy. Salad cream is permitted, in summer and even in the bottle, yet Daddies Sauce is unspoken of and HP Sauce is considered lower than almost anything you can think of, lower even than Camp Coffee. This, from a man who drinks Mateus Rosé.

I am not quite sure on what my father bases his larder snobbery. He prefers Crosse & Blackwell to Heinz (which he thinks is a bit common) except where salad cream is concerned and mustard must always be English and from

Norwich, never French. He bought a jar of mayonnaise once from the food hall in Beatties but said it was too oily. And of course it was French.

Tea is never, ever Typhoo or Brooke Bond. PG Tips is beyond the pale and the monkeys in drag who advertise it haven't helped. Tea in our house is Twinings. Pity he calls it Twinnings as in winnings. Coffee was Maxwell House but is now something called Bird's Mellow, which Joan tried when she found a coupon in *Woman's Journal*. 'Mmmm, it's so smooth,' she cooed, and from then on it'd be Bird's Mellow every time.

Dad and I refuse to eat margarine. Joan will only eat Blue Band Soft, which spreads without tearing the bread. We keep the butter in a yellow butter dish made from thick plastic, which matches exactly the yellow-and-white check table mats in the kitchen. On the rare occasion we eat in the dining room we get out the cork-backed mats with hunting scenes on them. Even a mug of coffee has to have a coaster. God help anyone who puts down a hot drink on the nest of tables.

We are all fond of tinned salmon. Either Princes or John West, which is mashed up with a little vinegar and always served with cucumber slices, again with a little vinegar. Tinned crab is Dad's favourite as are tinned pears. I love the syrup, which is thinner and less cloying than the stuff you get with peaches. We all like tinned apricots more than peaches.

We have always eaten tinned fruit with a tin of Nestlé's

cream, which we call Nessels, as in vessels. Since Joan has been on the scene we have something called Ideal Milk instead, which she calls 'Evap' and which ruins the fruit. I can tell Dad isn't keen, but he doesn't seem to mind as long as She likes it.

Everything seems to have changed of late. She's really into buttercream at the moment, which she makes with Rayner's vanilla essence, icing sugar and Blue Band Soft. At the weekend we now get Cornish Ice Cream instead of Arctic Roll and Dairy Box instead of Black Magic. I'm not allowed fizzy pop any more. I have to drink Tree Top or Robinson's Lemon Barley Water instead. Joan says that fizzy pop is too expensive.

Dad adores pickled walnuts. I adore the way Joan shudders as he cuts into the browny black blobs. We haven't had tripe for a while. Joan doesn't like the smell. But we do have boiled neck of lamb stew, which smells ten times worse than tripe. But she likes that. So we have it.

Coffee and Walnut Cake

Mrs Jones lived in a granny flat next to her daughter's house on Collins Green. It was more of a garden shed actually but comfy enough with its collection of framed photos, china ornaments on crocheted doilies and lone aspidistra. Mrs Jones was dying to the ticking of a grandfather clock. Her daughter made cake. Lemon cake, date cake, chocolate cake, aniseed cake, cherry cake, walnut cake, round cake, square cake, plain cake, fancy cake. Best of all she made coffee cake, thick, light sponge the colour of milky coffee, with nubbly bits of walnut in and two thick layers of walnut frosting. I would love to say I went to see old Mrs J. every week to cheer up a lonely old lady, but I cannot. I went for the cake.

I made a habit of knocking on Miss Jones's door just to say I was popping in to see her mother. This was, you understand, to let her know I was visiting, not to instigate the delivery of cake and lemonade.

One Tuesday visit had included two slices of particularly wonderful coffee cake, and I figured there would be still be some left the following day. I knocked at the door but it was already open. I called her name, then peered inside. A neat hallway, a kitchen sink, clearly visible, full of cake tins and mixing bowls. Suddenly something hit me from behind and I fell forward on to my hands and knees. Before I could call out a single word two huge paws slipped around my shoulders, two hind legs tucked behind mine, and the smooth chest of Miss Jones's pet Alsatian pushed down on my back. I froze, waiting for his teeth to sink into my neck. Instead, I just felt something cold and wet against the top of my bare leg.

The humping – frantic, breathy, his wet tongue lolloping against my ear – seemed to last for ever. Part of me wanted Miss Jones to come round the corner and rescue me, but another part didn't. I would rather no one, least of all a sixty-year-old spinster with a tea tray in her hand, witnessed a sex-starved Alsatian pumping away at me like a sailor on leave. Especially when I was wearing short trousers.

I loved that cake dearly, as I do to this day, but never again did I visit that dear old lady or eat coffee and walnut cake to the sound of a ticking grandfather clock.

Candyfloss

Joan wants to go on holiday but doesn't fancy Bournemouth. She says it's la-di-da. Dad suggests Tenby but she doesn't fancy that either. I'm not allowed to suggest anywhere.

Joan has talked Dad into going to Blackpool. She has been before and thinks he might like it. I don't like to point out to her that that is rather like thinking he might take to pigeon-fancying or drinking milk stout. As we start the long drive towards our summer holiday on the golden mile the look on my father's face is as sour as the sherbet lemons Joan keeps passing over to him. I think he's embarrassed. At one point there is silence in the car for over two hours. It is broken only because Dad wants to stop to go to the loo. Or, as he puts it, 'to go and see a man about a dog'.

Blackpool turns out to be fun, but only if you enjoy hearing Scott McKenzie singing 'If you're going to San ... Fran ... cisco' blaring from every shop from dawn to dusk.

Which I did. Joan permanently looks like she's about to say sorry I brought you here, though she never actually does. Dad spends the entire week looking like he'd rather be somewhere, anywhere, else. 'They must all be on drugs,' he mutters when a bare-chested guy with long blond hair and orange flares dances along the front pinging a pair of finger-cymbals in people's ears.

I can't remember ever having such a good time. Dad's pissed off with Joan for dragging him to somewhere that sells kiss-me-quick hats and saucy postcards, she's caked in guilt because she knows he's hating every second of it. I'm wondering what it would be like to be stoned and wishing I could have a flowery shirt like every other male in Blackpool. (Except my dad, of course, who is wearing a check shirt, brown brogues, a tie and a sort of waistcoat with a suede front.) 'Don't be so stupid,' snaps Dad when I ask if I can have a flowery shirt from one of the shops on the front. 'Everyone will think you're a fairy.'

We have two rooms at a bed and breakfast just off the main drag. 'It will be quieter here.' There is one room for Joan and another for Dad and me. After dinner (ham salad, tinned peaches and cream), I lie there in the dark wondering if I nag them enough they'll let me have a flowery shirt tomorrow. I must be the only boy in Blackpool to be wearing grey shorts and a school pullover. Dad kneels by his bed and says his prayers as he always does. It amazes me that a man who can be so strict, fierce and cold actually thinks he has a right to speak to God. I thought people who prayed were gentle, meek and generous like Miss Martineau, the RE teacher at school, who once gave me a lift in the rain, or the giraffe-like Mr Gutteridge who took the daily service at Woodfield and sang hymns louder than I have ever heard anyone sing before or since. How can a man who puts the fear of God into his own child dare to get down on his knees and whisper sweet nothings into his hands? We both snuggle down and Dad puts the bedside light out with a loud click.

An hour later I'm still not asleep. If they won't let me have a paisley-patterned shirt, then I might buy the sea urchin bedside lamp that I saw in the lava lamp shop. I can't quite tell if Dad is still awake, but I guess he must be asleep because he hasn't moved an inch for the last fifteen minutes. The muffled giggles from the next room give way to the sound of not-so-muffled humping. The room is so dark that I can't see Dad, so he certainly can't see me. My hand wanders down the bedclothes and through the fly of my pyjama trousers. The humping gets louder, harder, and I try not to make the sheets rustle.

Next door finishes suddenly. In the unexpected silence that follows, my breathing becomes as piercing and clear as the smell of the little bar of Palmolive soap on the washbasin in the corner. Without warning, and as crisp as a bullet from a gun, Dad snaps, 'Stop it.'

We have breakfast in a neat room with stiff chairs, the white nets at the windows tied back with coloured ribbons.

Bacon and sausage for Joan and me, a kipper for Dad. I love the toast, which is cold and bendy and comes in a bent silver rack, just like it always does on holiday. The butter is hard and cold too. This is what I call hotel toast, very different from the hot, melting-butter stuff we get at home, but in its way just as good. There are plastic roses on the table in a thick, moulded glass vase. Dad says they are the ones you used to get free with Daz.

He seems more cheerful today, and lets me have my photograph taken with a monkey on my shoulder. He even cracks a joke about not being sure which one of us is which. I make several attempts at talking them into buying me something, anything, that might make me look like a hippie, but I get nowhere. In desperation I spend my pocket money on a small brass bell on a chain and hang it around my neck. We have lunch in a restaurant opposite the beach – battered haddock, chips and peas, followed by ice cream and tinned fruit cocktail. Dad has apple pie and custard. 'I think we'd better go home tomorrow,' he announces suddenly. 'I'm worried about leaving the greenhouse so long.'

Dad's usual obsession with people being 'one of them' had now turned to people being 'on drugs'. The signs, according to my father, were anyone whose hair touched their collar or who failed to wear socks with their sandals. Though the real clincher was a shoulder bag. By my reckoning this meant pretty much everyone in Blackpool. Except, of course, us.

Late in the afternoon, Joan suddenly appears with a stick of vivid pink candyfloss. 'He's got to try it, Tony, everyone eats it here.' We take a last embarrassed walk along the front, my father three paces ahead of me, pretending to be nothing to do with the young son trailing behind him. The one in the beige V-neck and tinkling hippie bell, tucking into a vast nest of shocking-pink candyfloss.

The Man in the Woods

The school bus drops me at the bottom of the hill and I walk up, rain or shine. Sometimes I stop to pick primroses or to piss in the woods. Sometimes I scuff my shoes kicking the great piles of horse chestnut leaves that are pushed to the side of the road by the speeding cars, other times I just trudge up to the top.

I often dawdle, making up a story about how the coach broke down if Joan says anything about my being late. Today I walk parallel with the road but quite deep into the woods. There are a few last bluebells and the odd catkin, there are bright green leaves on the cobnuts and there are ramsons – wild garlic – underfoot. Even with all this new young growth, there is something slightly sinister about the woods. It's like someone is always watching you.

There are often crackles as you walk. Rabbits usually and sometimes squirrels. My father tells me it's probably a yeti or a one-armed man like the Fugitive. The crackling twigs are heavier than usual today, but they've gone quiet now. I don't normally come this deep into the woods. Suddenly I catch a glimpse of a man, a tall man with long hair, about twenty or twenty-five, with tight faded jeans and a tweed jacket with elbow patches. He's just standing there by the trunk of a tree, partly covered by the thin branches of a young cobnut bush, looking down at the ground. He's got his dick out, like he is having a pee.

But he's not peeing. He's wanking, slowly sliding his hand back and forth, his jacket pulled right back with his other hand, allowing me a perfect view. I am not sure whether I should run or stay. I want to watch what he's doing but my breathing is so loud and I'm starting to tremble. He seems oblivious to me, though I must be only ten feet away. There are prickles on the back of my neck, just under my hairline.

He carries on, a little faster now. Then suddenly he glances my way, for a second, maybe even less, then carries on. I think he's seen me. I'm not sure. I want to cough, my mouth is so dry. I wet my lips with my tongue. My mouth tastes furry. Slowly, the man turns his head towards me and looks straight at me. Then he turns his whole body to face me, still wanking. He motions to me, impatiently with his head, his eyebrows furrowed. His face is young, like the guy in the Small Faces, but his skin is darker, like he spends more time out of doors. I give a tiny smile, a quivering smile, and start to walk away. I'm shaking properly now and my tummy's turning over and over and there's a bitter taste in my mouth. I take big steps over the mossy logs and into the brambles, clutching my satchel to my side to stop it catching on the twigs. The man is about six feet behind me and taking huge strides towards me. The twigs snap loudly. I'm almost at the road but there's a wide wet patch, like a shallow pool, in the way and the ground is getting boggy. I'm trying to walk on tiptoe. Suddenly my left foot comes out of its shoe. I sort of hop-leap the last bit of water and slip, but only slightly, on the dry bank, then right myself. I'm on the road now and there's the sound of a lorry whining weakly in the distance. My foot touches the tarmac and I suddenly feel safe. I glance behind me without stopping. The man has gone. I walk on, hot and red and itchy, wondering how I am going to explain to Joan about the shoe.

Walnut Whip 1

Some chocolate bars were considered adult territory. They were not labelled as such and whether the chocolate was dark or light didn't really come into it. The distinction was more subliminal. After Eights, Terry's Chocolate Orange, Toblerone, Dark Chocolate Bounty (the one with the red wrapper), Bournville, Black Magic, Fry's Peppermint Cream, even Matchmakers were all considered as unsuitable for a young boy as watching an episode of ITV's raunchy *Armchair Theatre*.

Even kids' stuff had its limitations. Mars Bars and Topics were shrouded in some mysterious etiquette. My father used to cut his into slices, put them on a plate in a neat line and eat each piece like it was an expensive chocolate. That way, he could make a bar last through a whole episode of *The Avengers*. Putting any chocolate bar straight into my mouth was forbidden. Except, for some mysterious reason, a Milky Way. Obviously it was a size thing. I had to break off each piece of Mars with my fingers and pop it into my mouth. Biting it straight from the bar was probably enough to get me sent to my room. I am not quite sure what he would have done if I had sucked the chocolate off a Mars the way Joan did – wiggling the bar from side to side as she came to the end of each long, deeply explicit suck. There was something fascinating about watching the way the milky chocolate dissolved on her tongue and left little brown stains in the corner of her mouth.

When no one was looking I would take a Mars into the woods and suck off every last little bit of chocolate. Sometimes it would be a Fry's Crunchie instead, in which case I would bite off the end then worm away at the honeycomb centre with the tip of my tongue, seeing how much of the amber sugar filling I could get to dissolve before the chocolate around it collapsed. The sticky joy of the sugar and chocolate extended tenfold by the fact that I was eating in a manner quite acceptable to any normal parent.

One day my father brought home a handful of Walnut

Whips. I preferred the coffee flavour, Joan the plain chocolate one. While sucking a Flake was not permitted, sticking my tongue deep inside a Walnut Whip was. Not only was it allowed, it was considered a game for all the family. Each of us snapping off the walnut with our teeth, then breaking into the cone of chocolate and poking our tongues deep into the hollow. On a good day you could gouge out every scrap of sweet coffee-flavoured foam. You had to curl the edges of your tongue up to get it in, but you could happily get to the bottom. So thick was the chocolate shell on a Walnut Whip that there was no danger of it collapsing.

Friday night became Walnut Whip night. He would bring them out during the second commercial break in *The Persuaders*. So we'd all sit round watching Tony Curtis and Roger Moore, our tongues ferreting around inside our Walnut Whips. Quite why I was encouraged to practise this particular form of culinary cunnilingus, yet was barred from sucking a Mars bar, was something my father chose not to expand upon.

I learned to love the woods. Not ours with its neat rows of carefully pruned Christmas trees, but the woods further up the road, which were less dense and had chaotic mounds of brambles with more blackberries than you could eat. I would walk for hours at the weekends, coming back with Tupperware bowls of berries which Joan made into pies with Bramley apples from the old tree in the garden.

The woods were quiet; sometimes I would see no one all afternoon. It was here I would sit and read *Cordon Bleu* magazine or the cookery pages I tore out of Joan's *Woman's Journal*, and where I would masturbate, sometimes two or three times in an afternoon. Occasionally, I'd find pages torn from porn magazines that others had left there, pictures of big-breasted women with beehive hairdos and men with moustaches and medallions round their necks.

Dad continued buying us sweets to eat in the evenings. A Cadbury's Flake for Joan, a Toffee Crisp or Walnut Whip for me. He would usually just have an Aero and his pipe. My bedtime was at nine, even during the school holidays, and before that I had to take the dog out for his nightly walk. The road was narrow and the cars would come hurtling round the bends, often just missing me and the dog on his long lead. It seemed daft to take the dangerous route when it would be much safer to walk in the other direction, but I was forbidden from going up to the reservoir. 'It's not safe up there, the cars come at a hell of a pelt' was the old man's stern warning. In truth, the cars had a much clearer view of any pedestrian and the chances of being run down were much slimmer than the way I had been told to take.

I had no idea about the lay-by near the reservoir. I knew it existed, of course, and that at night cars would line up to look at the twinkling lights scattered round the Malvern Hills like diamonds in a necklace. On a frosty night you could see even further, each light sparkling in the cold night air that made your face feel like a peeled grapefruit. Tucked up watching the news, neither Dad nor Joan were likely to leave their chairs and no one would know if I took the reservoir route. And anyway, I could let the dog off his lead in the lay-by.

Once the lead was off I curled it up and stuffed it in my pocket, pulled apart the cellophane bag of Walnut Whip and bit off the walnut. I could see a row of cars all facing the glittering lights of the hamlets and villages below. The river shone like an abandoned silk scarf in the moonlight. People were sitting in their cars talking, some with their arms around each other. One car, a pale green-and-white Ford Capri, appeared to have no one in it, yet was swaying violently back and forth. A foot or two closer and I could see a pair of knees, wide apart, and then a slim, bare back. Within a foot of the car I got a view of a mechanically thrusting bottom.

I must have stayed there seven or eight minutes, heart pounding, mouth parched, licking the filling from my Walnut Whip, wishing it was an ice lolly and praying the dog would stay away. Then a car door opened on the other side of the lay-by and I ducked down by the driver's door of the Capri. A guy was standing with his back to me, peeing into the hedge. I couldn't believe how he couldn't hear my heart thumping. He got back into his car. The dog spotted me crouching and came scuttling towards me. I pushed him away then stopped when I could see he thought this was the start of some new game. The Capri suddenly stopped moving, I twisted my head round and looked gingerly up. Slowly, the driver's window opened an inch or two and a hand pushed something wet and glistening out of the window. It landed on my back, then, a second or two afterwards, a tissue followed. I shook myself, grabbed the dog by his collar and half ran, half walked, back down the hill, my heart hitting my ribcage, dropping the last bite of chocolate, the bit with the second walnut in it, behind me.

I was still panting when I pulled back the curtain that acted as the door to the cloakroom. 'All done then?' asked Dad as he walked over and I hoicked my jacket up on to an empty peg. Then, as the light from the kitchen door flashed into the dark world of coats and wellington boots, he peered over the top of his bifocals and asked, 'What's THAT on the back of your jacket?'

'Oh, that ruddy dog,' I said, my stomach doing a sick-making somersault. 'He's been slobbering everywhere again,' and I discreetly wiped a thick, shining line of semen off the back of my school blazer.

The Hostess Trolley

My aunt and uncle are coming for Christmas. Dad has decided to buy a hostess trolley so we can have Boxing Day tea in the sitting room. Not one of the dinky variety that is actually no more than three tin trays with wheels and a pram handle, but the full bells and whistles number, about six feet long with a middle shelf that glides up on a spring to form a table with the top shelf. It weighs a ton. With its walnut veneer it is the sort of hostess trolley for which one needs an HGV licence.

After much debate, it is decided that the hostess trolley is to live for the rest of the year in the dining room. This will necessitate lifting it up the step from the dining room into the hall, down the step to the sitting room, down another step to the kitchen then, this time fully laden, back up to the sitting room. As labour-saving devices go this is not one of Dad's better ideas.

Auntie Elvie and Uncle Len have little time for Joan, but adore my father, who is my aunt's younger brother and whom she had, in effect, brought up.

Dad is worried that they think Joan is a 'gold-digger' and is anxious that all will go well.

They are given Joan's room overlooking 'the view' and she takes mine. Dad and I have to double up in his bed, which I hate because it smells of the cortisone cream he uses on his nettle rash.

Joan does us proud. Displayed on the top tier of the trolley, there's ham with tomato water lilies, tinned salmon with wafer-thin cucumber in vinegar, a dish of sliced beetroot, salad cream in a sauce boat and a veal and ham pie with an egg in the middle. There's a plate of radishes, a dish of cress and even a pickle fork for the pickled onions. 'The tongue's for your father,' she pipes, as if anyone else would touch the stuff. On the second tier is one of Dad's trifles with flaked almonds and tiny yellow balls on top, a plate of home-made mince pies and a jelly with mandarin orange segments in it. And, of course, there's The Cake. After thirty years of marriage Elvie can only cook chops and frozen beans so is understandably impressed by it all. 'She does a wonderful spread,' says Elvie, her back getting straighter with every syllable.

Joan, Dad, Uncle Len and me all take a leg each and try to lift the trolley with its splendid array up the kitchen step. The trifle slides threateningly, one of the tomato water lilies falls off the ham. We decide it will be safer to unload the trolley and carry it up the step and into the sitting room, then bring all the food from the kitchen and place it on the shelves. Dad looks faintly embarrassed that the trolley has actually made more work rather than less. He pulls the toggle that allows the lower tier – trifle, cake, mince pies, jelly and, now, a Cadbury's chocolate cake too – to glide up and join the top tier to make a vast table. We all go 'ooooo' at the appropriate moment.

Just as Dad is passing round the plates and I am handing round parcels of napkins containing the knives, forks and spoons, the toggle that supports the shelves pops out of its housing and the whole trolley collapses, throwing ham, salad cream, trifle and beetroot all over the carpet. Only the cake survives unscathed.

'Oh, bugger, bugger and bugger again,' snaps Dad. We all rush to pick everything up, slapping it all back on plates and into bowls, though we decide to give up on the salad cream for which Joan fetches a wet dishcloth.

'No, no, don't fuss,' soothes Elvie, 'it'll be fine,' as she wipes a dollop of whipped cream off the slice of boiled ham on her plate. Later, as we all silently play with our food, carefully inspecting it for dog hairs and carpet fluff, I watch my aunt wince as she politely swallows a spoonful of trifle I know very well has a pickled onion in it.

Walnut Whip 2

The trips to the lay-by had become a nightly thing. I'd grab my Walnut Whip, the dog and head off to the lay-by. Fridays and Saturdays were busiest, so much so I had to make up stories about the dog refusing to 'go' to explain my ever-lengthening trips. Once, when the occupants of every car seemed to be going at it, I was so long I had to tell them the dog had run off and I had spent the last hour looking for him.

Saturday afternoon, late summer, and Dad tells me to come for a walk. He does this, every now and again. No doubt another futile attempt to get me to accept Joan, to let her into my life.

'I want to know what's up with you. Joan does everything she can to make you happy,' he says as we get to the end of the garden and start to climb up towards the reservoir. 'She looks after you like you were her own son. Yet you mope around with a long face if she asks you to do anything, you don't speak to her unless she speaks to you first, and you didn't even remember her birthday. She's very fond of you and you just throw it back in her face.'

I have heard it all before. He just doesn't get it. He is so in love with this woman he can't see anything but good in her. He doesn't see her piercing eyes and mean little mouth, the way she used him, and me, to claw her way out of her tawdry little life. How she has taken over, pushing me around, trying to model me into some creep who keeps his sock drawer tidy and carries a clean handkerchief. He doesn't see, cannot see, her cold, calculating eyes or the unnatural demands she makes of a teenage boy ('tidy your room, tidy your drawers, don't put pictures on the wall, don't play your records so loud, do your homework, polish your shoes, use a plate, use a coaster, use a napkin, use a hanky, don't slam the door, don't tease the dog, rinse the bath, wash your hands, STOP MAKING SMELLS'). This man is so besotted he hasn't even noticed she has changed our soft, cuddly cotton sheets for easy-care polyester cotton. All he sees is warm ironing and apple crumble.

I don't say anything for a while. I'm not sure what there is to say. I am a nuisance, a thorn in the lovebirds' sides. His own son is in the way. A constant reminder of the wife he so dearly loved and yet so desperately wants to forget. 'I don't know what you mean, everything's fine,' I say quietly. We are up by the woods now.

'Just try a little bit, will you? I know she's not Mummy, but she's here and if you don't like it you'll have to go into care.'

Into care. I'd heard him say that before, many years ago, when we were walking across the fields and I thought Mum was telling him she was going to have a baby when she was actually telling him she was going to die. Getting rid of me has apparently always been an option. 'Everything's fine,' I repeat, head down now.

'One more thing and that's it, all right,' he warns. 'I've had enough.'

Suddenly Dad swings left into the lay-by. We walk along the tarmac towards the stile that would lead us into the long field. Half of Worcestershire is laid out before us; the churches and their ancient cemeteries, little clusters of cottages, acre upon acre of hop fields. Such a magical, secret place at night, by day the lay-by looks shabby, and shockingly real. Dad's eyes drop to the ground and suddenly his brow puckers like someone has drawn a hot iron over a pair of silk knickers. I can feel the colour working its way up my neck and into my ears; hot, red, embarrassed. In the cold light of day there are no twinkling stars and distant lights, no naked bottoms, no spread legs, no muffled cries. Just hundreds of used condoms, little piles of dog shit and dozens upon dozens of Walnut Whip wrappers.

Happy Families

Dad honestly believes he has created a storybook happy family, that lives in a pretty cottage with roses round the door. A neatly dressed, polite teenager, a 'mum' who cooks like an angel and a dad who does dad-type things like bringing home the bacon, chopping logs for the fire and filling a greenhouse with tomatoes and begonias. Dad, you are living in a fantasy world.

I would dearly like to take him aside and point out a few facts that seem to have escaped his attention. Like the fact that his neatly dressed, polite son has never been so lonely in his entire life; that the woman he thinks loves him just used him to escape from the poor hand she was dealt; that the happy family he imagines he has created is nothing more than a sham. I would also like to bring up the fact that this woman of his (yes, his, not mine) is making my life a misery with her ever-increasing demands for tidiness, cleanliness, punctuality and general good behaviour. (This is more like life in the army than a normal childhood.) That the more I agree to her ridiculous demands (apparently she plans to tell Dad I should look for a part-time job so I can pay 'rent' to live in my own home) the more obscene her demands become.

In passing I might also mention the small fact that she hasn't a good word to say about anybody, including my dad, her own daughters (one of whom has stood by her through thick and thin), all of our relatives, who she thinks are 'snobs', and certainly not the neatly dressed and polite little boy she was originally employed to look after. And if I could ever get his attention I might just point out that listening to records and watching TV and spending time in my room is what I do because there is nothing else to do in this sodding, wretched wilderness he has brought us to.

I could bring up a few other matters:

1. Farting is perfectly normal in a boy of my age, as is burping and leaving 'snail-trails' on his sheets.
2. Normal boys of my age do not have to empty the bin in their bedroom every day, fold the towels in the bathroom perfectly after use or put their dirty clothes in the laundry basket.
3. It is not normal for boys to rinse their wellingtons every time they take them off.
4. No other boy I know has to do either the washing up or the drying after every meal; take the dog out every day; collect the eggs from the farm; get back from school at exactly the right time and help with the gardening after school.
5. All the other boys I know are allowed to make a mess, be untidy, run around, make noise, have friends round and put posters up on their bedroom wall.
6. Most of the boys I know are just allowed to be boys.

Here, Dad, is a list of the things she says get on her nerves: me kicking a ball against the garden wall, me watching TV when it's sunny outside, me drinking my pop too quickly, me burping after drinking my pop too quickly, me wiping my mouth with the back of my hand after drinking pop too quickly, me putting on clean clothes every day, me not putting on clean clothes every day, me sitting down and talking to her when she's having a cigarette, me not sitting down with her when she's having a cigarette, me not helping when she's cooking, me getting in her way when she's cooking, me hanging around when she's trying to work, me going out to play when she's trying to work, me going up to my room, me not going up to my room, me being in all the time, me being out all the time.

I can do NOTHING right for this woman Dad has brought into our lives. I hate her and I hate him for loving her. And what is more, I don't think slippers were a suitable birthday present for a fourteen-year-old.

Rabbit

Joan's acts of kindness came at you like car headlights, momentarily blinding you on a long, dark, lonely road. Like when she hid from my father the fact I had got 9 per cent in my mock maths O level. 'He doesn't need to know, I don't think he's very good at maths either.' Or the time she helped me search for Dad's new Parker fountain pen which I had borrowed and lost on the way to school. When we found it, its shiny maroon cap smashed to smithereens on the roadside, she lent me the money secretly to buy a replacement.

One morning I went up the garden to feed my rabbit to find his cage door wide open and two of the dogs from the farm playing tug-of-war with him. I didn't look too closely, I just saw one dog at either end of the long white body, growling, teeth bared, the rabbit's fur already smeared on one side with blood. The two dogs, Jack Russells, just pulled and pulled like they had either end of a bone. The rabbit seemed so long now, even longer than the ones hanging on the three iron hooks outside the butcher's. I ran back indoors, shaking. I wanted to shout and shriek, but knew Joan would get cross if I raised my voice in the house. Instead, I just ran upstairs, knocked on her door and told her what was happening.

Joan ran up the garden path in her dressing gown, lashing out at the dogs with the plastic broom. I saw them run off and watched in tears as Joan picked up two separate lumps of white body. She came back, the broom still in her right hand, and wrapped her left arm around my shoulder. She had never done that before. Later, when I was still too upset to bury the pieces, she dug a hole under the horse chestnut tree and dropped them into it, covering the mangled remains with soil. 'We'll get a rose and plant it on top,' she said. Then she got out the white paint she used to cover the moss on the outside wall and I wrote his name in neat letters on a piece of wooden apple crate. The first few letters were too large, and frankly a bit wonky, and though the letters got smaller there was no room to finish the inscription. Dear old Ringo Rabbit ended up being buried as Ringo Rabbi. 'Never mind, we'll get him a bigger gravestone tomorrow,' she said, but we never did.

Damson Jam

'It isn't just about making scones for tea,' said Miss Adams, straight-backed, cold and rather old for her years, as she introduced the cookery syllabus to the Wednesday class. Beverly Brown, kind, round and pumpkin-faced, deflated instantly like a burst balloon. The lovely Dee Hanratty whispered 'Good' behind her hand, 'I hate sultanas.' I suddenly got nervous, wondering just how difficult my first cookery lessons were going to be. Did Miss Adams mean we were going to be boning whole lambs and making soufflés then? 'We will be doing everything from cooking rice to costing entire meals,' she warned, her voice getting higher with every word. The word rice put the fear of God into me. I'd never even eaten the stuff, let alone cooked it.

The first lesson, a week later, couldn't have been easier. My Victoria sandwich rose like a dream and had, according to Miss Adams, a perfect 'crumb' and a fine flavour. Even Beverly, who was obviously born both to bake and eat the results, was impressed. I lowered my sugar-topped success into a Peak Frean's biscuit tin and squeezed it into my duffel bag for the journey home.

I couldn't wait to show my father, who for all his disinterest couldn't fail to congratulate me. He was late as people always are on occasions like this. I kept looking at the clock, desperate for him to come home. To see and smell my cake. To eat it. The cake had been sitting on the kitchen table, Joan sitting next to it smoking Embassy after Embassy, occasionally glancing in the direction of my cake.

'Look at that!' said my father, obviously as proud as punch despite everything. 'Isn't that a beauty?'

'Hmm,' said Joan abruptly, swishing her head to the left and blowing out a last cloud of smoke. She then tightened her lips into a straight line and stubbed out her cigarette in the Royal Worcester ashtray like she was trying to squash a cockroach.

The following week we all took damsons to make jam. I had picked mine from the tree that overhung the maze of hedges around the water pump. It was pure coincidence that it was my father's favourite, not to mention mine. Miss Adams had made us read the preserving chapter in 'O' Level Cookery by Phyllis Abbey, the red one with the pie on the front. I knew it almost word for word. While the girls got away with as little as they could, I read everything in sight. After all, I had three years of missed lessons and the Fablon-topped coffee table I made in woodwork to make up for.

We strained the jam, thick and royal purple, into warm jars, let it cool, then cut out perfect discs of greaseproof paper and smoothed them on to the surface of each jar. We stretched over tight little cellophane covers and held them in place with blue rubber bands, then neatly wrote out our names and the date and the proud words 'Home-Made Damson Jam'.

The bus took ages to wind its way through Wichenford, Broadheath, Broadwas, eventually pulling up outside the Talbot Hotel at Knightwick. 'Can't go any further today,' boomed Mr Chater. 'Brakes are a bit funny. You'll have to walk up the hill yourself.' A full satchel and a duffel bag full of jam is enough to carry down the aisle of the bus let alone up a one-in-six hill. The pots clanked in my bag. I got to the top, hot and anxious that some of Dad's precious jam might have spilled.

Joan had been busy in the garden, the drive and lawn swept of last week's fallen leaves, the edges of the lawn trimmed like a choirboy's fringe, every blob of green yuk scooped from the top of the pond. It wouldn't have surprised me if she had polished the orange berries on the cotoneaster. Inside, every surface shone; there were spider-petalled dahlias, bright yellow and maroon and white in a jade green vase on the table. The smell of baking hung in the air like a soft, warm blanket. There were jam tarts, lemon curd tarts and butterfly cakes. There was a lattice-topped mince pie as big as a plate, and in the bottom tier of the stackable see-through cake 'tins' was a sponge, light, golden and sparkling with caster sugar. It was filled with a thick layer of damson jam.

Wednesday now became Joan's baking day. Each week I would proudly come home from school with a flask of vegetable soup, a sunken fruit cake, a box of eclairs (hideously squashed by Roger Mountford's satchel) or, on one occasion, an apple meringue pie whose filling had run out over the bottom of the tin, to find the house full of warm ironing, a freshly brushed dog and enough cakes, tarts and pies to feed the entire village.

Tears

Joan is sitting on the garden hammock, swinging back and forth under its tasselled shade. She's been crying. I ask her what's wrong and she shows me a birthday card from one of the disabled women she used to visit. It says simply:

I hope you are happy with your new life
From your friend Sarah

And then in brackets:

(Not dead, but forgotten.)

Joan is clearly hurt. The truth is that she hasn't forgotten Sarah or any other of the disabled people she used to go and see. She talks about them all the time, and I know she would go and see them if she could, but she doesn't drive and Dad doesn't seem to want to take her back there. Not even for the day. I am not sure he wants to let her out of his sight. Later, I see the card in the bin, torn in two.

Joan has been quite pensive of late. I know she is hurt by the fact that two of her daughters haven't spoken to her since the day she came to live with my father and that she hasn't seen any of her sisters for at least four years. She is aware, I know, that none of my dad's friends likes her. It suddenly occurs to me that she is probably as lonely as I am.

Toast 2

'I want to talk to you about something,' says my father ominously and with one of those smiles that somehow manages to both scare and patronise me all at once. We walk out into the garden and round the rose beds, him pretending to look closely at each pink-edged Peace rose, me silently cringing, hoping desperately he isn't about to say 'man to man'.

'I've asked your Auntie Joan to marry me and she's said yes,' he says in a calm no-messing sort of a way, squishing a greenfly between his thumb and forefinger as he does so and wiping it off on his trousers. 'I think she's just like Mummy, don't you?'

I just stand there, intently examining a fully open rose, not knowing what to say. Mummy hadn't ever smoked or said 'bleedin'. Neither had she cleaned houses for a living or bought clothes from a catalogue. I don't think she had ever set foot in C&A let alone bought a coat from there. Mummy never wore mascara, or perfume bought from a woman who came to the door, or walked around in a quilted nylon 'housecoat'. I had never seen Mum with curlers in her hair or putting her lipstick on at the table. Neither had I ever heard her say 'arse'.

Mummy hadn't drunk snowballs or collected cigarette coupons, she had never cut tokens from the back of packets or stuck Green Shield Stamps in a book. Mum had never played bingo and didn't have yellow nicotine stains on her fingers. I am sure she would never have worn anything made of brushed nylon. (Mum wore mushroom-coloured clothes and had shoes and handbags that always matched. I had never seen her without a brooch. Mum always said 'touch wood' after she had tempted fate and 'bless you' if I sneezed or farted. She said 'oh heck!' rather than 'bugger, bugger, bugger'.)

Mummy never used my father as a threat to get me to do what she wanted, neither did she hug me when he was looking yet freeze me out when he wasn't. Mummy had never had a 'blue rinse' put in her hair or clear varnish on her nails. Mummy never said 'nigger brown'. Mummy never used air freshener.

I just keep staring at the rose, the petals, the long yellow stamens, stem, the fat red thorns, wanting to say so much. Wanting to tell him how the woman he is going to marry nags me from the moment I get up in the morning till I go to bed; how she makes me wash up my mug the second I have finished my coffee, dry it and immediately put it away in the cupboard; how she always makes me write out shopping lists and fill in forms for her because she says, 'I haven't got my right glasses on'; how it takes her a good five minutes to sign her name on his birthday card, leaving a gap between each letter. And how sometimes we have to start again because she gets it wrong. I am desperate to tell him how I caught her looking through the files in his desk marked 'bank statements' and how she once said she couldn't wait to get back to where she came from, only this time 'I'll have my own house, not one off the council.'

Most of all I want to tell him how she won't let me make toast when I come in from school, how she says it is because I will make crumbs and she has spent all day 'cleaning his bleeding kitchen'.

I want to tell him that there is no one on this earth less like Mummy.

The Wedding Cake

Dad's eyes filled with tears when he saw the wedding cake. He seemed as shocked as I was at my handiwork. We stood there, his arm around my shoulders, admiring the three layers of cake held up with eight white columns, the perfectly flat, snow-white icing with its diamond trellis motifs and the bride and groom standing proudly on top. I had used Mum's Christmas cake recipe, still folded neatly in the bowl of the food mixer, and borrowed the largest tin from Miss Jones down the road. The templates for the swags and curls had come from a cake-decorating manual I had borrowed from the mobile library, the shell edging and the piped legend 'Joan and Tony' were learned by practising with a piping set I had bought with my pocket money last time I went to town.

I felt like I was glowing from the inside out. I bit my bottom lip to stop the tears coming when Dad hugged me and said he had never imagined it would look so beautiful. Joan said, 'You made a good job of that, didn't you, lad?' and promptly put a tea towel over it. She said it was 'to keep the dust off till Saturday'.

It was a small ceremony, on a sunny spring day with daffodils and cherry blossom blooming in the register office garden, a surprisingly jolly affair considering the wave of disapproval from our side of the family. There were my uncles, Ron and Freddie, and my lovely Auntie Hilda, all in good spirits despite the occasion, brother John and Elvie, Dad's cantankerous older sister who came, one assumes, only to scoff at the hat she had given Joan as a wedding present. A vast beribboned turban festooned in trellis and petals that bore more than a passing resemblance to the wedding cake. My other brother and his wife Stevie drove up from Cornwall in their Alfa-Romeo. Dressed coolly in blue-black suits they were more forgiving of my father's choice of wife than the rest of us, but rather less so of The Hat.

On Joan's side was her youngest daughter Mary, the only one still speaking to her, with her husband Martin, a panel beater; her older sister Rose, more solidly built than Joan and who claimed to hear sparrows in her head, and brother-in-law Arnold, who Joan reckoned would 'turn up to the opening of a packet of Woodbines if there was a free meal in it'.

The free meal was a dip in the 'running buffet' at the Hundred House in Great Whitley. (Cold roast beef, quiche, potato salad and more puddings than a WI cookbook.) Rose tasted her first – and probably last – chocolate roulade. Arnold politely refused the quiche as he said foreign food always upset his stomach. He made up for it with the Charlotte russe. As we drove back to the house, me sitting in silence in the back of the car, I realised I had never seen either Dad or Joan looking happier. Though I suspected each of them was happy for entirely different reasons.

Duckling à l'orange

'Well, as it happens we do need a bit of help on Friday and Saturday nights,' said Wing Commander Howard, wiping beer froth from his moustache. 'Can you start tomorrow?'

The Talbot was an old black-and-white coaching inn at the bottom of the hill and so close to the River Teme the cellars used to flood in winter. We popped in sometimes on a Saturday on the way back from shopping in Bromyard, getting there early so we could hog the polished wooden settles that framed the vast fireplace. Dad would order the ploughman's of Cheddar, cottage loaf and a tomato. Joan and I would have scampi in the basket and a 'half' of lemon and lime.

'How much is he paying you?' snapped a suddenly cross Joan, eavesdropping, as I told Dad I had been offered a job.

'He didn't say,' I shrugged. 'He just said he'd look after me.'

'Don't worry, he'll be all right, I'm sure the old chap's as good as his word,' volunteered Dad.

Joan pursed her lips. 'I've never heard anything like it, not telling someone how much they are going to be paid. A boy as well.'

Wing Commander Howard wasn't there when I walked into the bar; just a middle-aged woman with a soft perm and a mouth like a pickled onion. I hung around for a minute or two then walked out again and stood by the phone box in the car park, waiting to catch him as he arrived. I was too early anyway. As it got closer to seven o'clock I gave up and went round the back of the hotel and knocked on the glass door.

'Yes, what is it?' yelled a plump, smiling woman with a pudding-basin haircut, wiping her hands on the front of her apron.

'I'm supposed to start work in the kitchen tonight. Are you Diane?'

Diane told me she had just been promoted to head cook. 'No, there's just me,' she replied when asked how many people worked under her, 'and you now, I suppose.' She glanced down at my shoes, specially polished for the occasion and laughed, 'You'd better get an apron. I'll show you round.'

'This is the freezer where we keep the main courses.' She lifted the battered white lid of the chest freezer to reveal several open cardboard boxes stuffed with plastic pouches labelled Duckling a l'Orange, Boeuf Bourguignon and Coq au Vin, then she pointed to another, 'That's the Veal Cordon Bleu. That's the most expensive.' The words Alveston Kitchens were printed on every packet in curly type under an outline of a chef's hat. 'When Wing Commander or Mrs H. brings in an order you come up and get the main courses, then bring them down to me to cook. Can you manage that?' Di smiled a fat, watermelon smile. 'I've defrosted a pâté de campagne for tonight, but sometimes we get through two. Oh, and there's the prawns for the prawn cocktail. We've only got eight booked tonight so I'll have time to show you everything as we go, unless we get a lot of "casuals" in.'

Steaks, salmon and the mixed grill (for whose vast

portions the restaurant was renowned) were the only main courses that didn't come from a plastic bag. The salmon was frozen but Diane did it herself, cleaning and cutting up a whole one and freezing it the day it came in. 'Locals mostly, they bring it back from a day on the river. My Harry goes sometimes. The vegetables tonight are runner beans and cauliflower cheese, sometimes I do courgettes or leeks in white sauce.' I liked Diane instantly. 'Oh, and remind me to show you how to make toast to go with the pâté.'

That night I went home having sliced runner beans, been shown how to garnish a slice of pâté with an orange twist and a sprig of parsley, how to tell a frozen coq from a frozen duck when the label comes off by feeling the shape of the leg through the plastic, and how to cut a slice of lemon so that it hooks neatly on to a wine glass of prawn cocktail. I knew how to pipe a swirly rosette of cream on the side of a slice of fruit pie, how to tell if an avocado is ripe and how to defrost prawns really quickly when you have forgotten to take them out of the freezer (put the bag in the sink and run the hot tap over them).

'I hope he paid you,' said Joan curtly when I bounced in at eleven-thirty, bursting to tell them everything I had done on my first night. He hadn't, but would at the end of the week he said. Frankly, I didn't care if he never paid me. I had never enjoyed myself so much in my life. Even Joan's snipe of 'Go and have a bath, you stink of frying' just bounced off me like water droplets off a cabbage leaf. I had made prawn cocktail (three actually), piped a whole tray of duchesse potatoes and put chopped parsley on the duckling à l'orange exactly at the moment that Diane had squeezed the leg and its glossy marmalade-scented sauce from its hot plastic sachet. I had made fingers of toast for the pâté and defrosted a Black Forest gâteau (though no one had actually had any). Bugger Joan, bugger Daddy, bugger everyone. At last I was a chef.

I stomped up the stairs to my room, hot, sticky and excited, and stood with my back against the cold wood of the bedroom door. I almost didn't hear Joan shouting from the bottom of the stairs, 'And don't forget to put your dirty clothes in the Ali Baba.'

Fillet and Rump

'Fillet's a bit more tender,' said Di, on whose every word I now hung. 'Rump's more interesting. We get through a lot of fillet on a Saturday night. It's the Gin and Jag set, they won't touch rump. More money than sense, of course.'

Di was teaching me more in two evenings a week than Miss Adams had managed in a whole year of domestic science lessons, or home economics as they had recently decided to call it. I was working Sundays too now, when there was a choice of three roasts on the menu – a rolled rib of beef the size of a tree trunk, chicken, lamb and occasionally pork – and the odd night during the week.

Di's Yorkshire pudding was as high as I had ever seen, even more billowing and cloud-like than Joan's. The first time I saw it I couldn't wait to get home to mouth off about it.

Di taught me how to make gravy so that it shone and roast potatoes that were golden and crunchy outside and melting within. One Sunday lunch, when the Howards weren't around she taught me how to grill rump and fillet, 'they might ask you to do it on my night off', and how to do the onion rings in the deep-fat fryer to go with them. 'Flour, salt, pepper and straight into the bubbling oil. You can't have a steak without onion rings.'

'The people on table four are going to be the new owners, go on, have a peep,' said Di one Saturday evening towards the end of term. 'They came in earlier and introduced themselves to me. Doreen and Ken. I don't know how they're going to get on here, they've never had a restaurant before, but they seem keen enough. They're used to running a farm.'

Doreen Beckett, slim, red hair, freckles, as unlike a farmer's wife as you could ever imagine, took over the running of the restaurant and the rooms, keeping a firmer eye on the expenses and waste than had the Howards. Her jockey-sized husband Ken took root in the public bar and never budged again. Their son Stuart was either at drama school or at the Royal Ballet School, depending on which one of his parents you asked. In fairness to Mr Beckett, not many of his farming mates can have had a son at ballet school. He's so beautiful, announced Doreen, he'll be a star one day.

The more time I spent with Doreen and Diane and the less with Joan the happier I was. During the summer holiday I worked both lunch and dinner, staying put in the afternoons polishing the silver and laying up the dining room. 'I don't know why you don't take your bed down there,' snarled Joan one night when I came in sticky and smelly from grilling steaks. 'You might as well bleedin' live down there.'

The kitchen looked out on to the gravel car park and then to the wide field that led down to the river. 'No children in the bar' meant exactly that and they would often sit in the car park with pint glasses of lemonade while their parents drank in the lounge bar with its wood panels and hunting prints. There was one girl, older than the others, with piercing violet eyes and dark hair that straggled down over her shoulders, who would sit in the passenger seat of her parents' Humber Hawk for hours, sometimes reading, other times just staring out at the other kids. No one ever brought a drink out to her. Whenever the smoke of the grill – 'new order, table six, two rumps, one fillet and one mixed grill' – became unbearable I would stand in the car park with a lime and lemonade, or sometimes a shandy, and she would look up from her book and smile.

Whenever drinks were poured by mistake they were brought into the kitchen for the staff. By the end of the evening we had swigged our way through a rum old mixture of sweet Martini that had been mistaken for dry, cider poured from a bottle when the customer wanted draught and, best of all, gin and tonics when the customer just suddenly disappeared. In the sweat and smoke of the kitchen anything that came our way was welcome. Mr Beckett, ever under his wife's beady eye, would sometimes bring in a brandy and Babycham for Di, claiming it was a mistake. Funny there was always one about the same time each night.

One night a tray of drinks arrived in the kitchen – the result of someone doing a 'runner' – with only Diane and me to drink them. I took a couple of them out to the girl in the Humber, who received them with a smile that was cheeky, quizzical. She knocked them back like I had only ever seen anyone do on televison. Later, when I overcooked a steak and I hadn't got time to eat the evidence, I ran out into the car park with it, wrapped up in napkin, and gave her that too.

I started to watch out for Julia, at least I knew her name now if nothing else, and started cooking bits of fillet specially for her; the tail end perhaps, or a slice that had been cut too thin. 'Don't cook it so much next time,' she'd would say, with the same cheeky grin.

'I think someone fancies you,' said Diane one particularly sticky evening in late July. 'Your friend has been peeping at you all night.' And then, 'Go on, go and see her, I'll be all right if any orders come in.' I didn't like to tell Diane she was probably just looking for her supper.

And so it went on for three weeks, me sneaking drinks and medium-rare steaks to Julia in a soggy napkin, taking my breaks leaning against her car door, she talking to me through the open window while she tore off bits of steak.

Nights off were long, silent, intolerable. I would sit at home in the cold dining room, Joan watching *The Golden Shot* or *Randall & Hopkirk (Deceased)*, Dad out at one of his Masonic 'dos'. Only now it was the summer holidays and there was no homework, no excuse to be anywhere but sitting with her, or her and him, festering, while he sat in the chair in front of the telly, she on the floor snuggled between his legs. One night I lied about having to go to work, then walked down the hill to stand and talk to Julia all evening.

'Why don't we walk down to the river?' she asked. We walked, side by side and without speaking much, clambered over the stile and through the paddock towards the river and the oak tree whose roots came up through the mossy soil like a tangle of serpents.

We sat there, our backs flat against the trunk of the tree for an hour or more. Saying nothing much, picking up the odd acorn and chucking it at nothing in particular. At one point we said nothing for a good ten minutes. Welcome washes of cool breeze would come from nowhere, then disappear again leaving the air hot and heavy as lead. Still we said nothing. I wasn't sure what, if anything, I should be doing. In the lay-by I had seen more shagging than you could shake a stick at, but I wasn't sure what was supposed to happen before. I hadn't bothered to watch the cars where nothing much seemed to be going on. Then quietly, almost matter-of-factly, Julia just said, 'You'll have to hurry up. I've got to get back soon.'

We spent the remaining weeks of the summer holidays in a sort of steak-for-sex deal that seemed to suit both of us. Everyone called her my girlfriend, but she wasn't. It was just steak, snogging and shagging. Same place, same time. Life was pleasingly neat, tidy, predictable. I grilled steaks, stuffed prawn cocktails into wine goblets, defrosted coq au vin and learned to make Irish coffees, a thick layer of cream floating magically on the sweet, black, whiskey-laden coffee. I got into the habit of deliberately getting one wrong, the cream swirling down through the coffee just so I could have one before going off with Julia. I stashed away every penny of my wages in an old cigar box hidden behind my collection of the *Children's Encyclopaedia*. I saw Dad and Joan only long enough to walk through the sitting room on my way upstairs to bed and to pick up my perfectly ironed clothes from the airing cupboard. Neat, tidy, predictable. And then Stuart turned up.

Prawn Cocktail

There's something going on. Dad's wearing his best Rael Brook shirt and cavalry twills. Joan has come downstairs in the only thing she owns that didn't come from a catalogue. What is more, he is drinking a gin and tonic and she is holding a sweet Martini and lemonade. In the sink is a packet of prawns.

'Do you think they are defrosted yet?'

'I should think so, darling. I took them out an hour ago.'

He turns to me. 'We thought we'd have prawn cocktail tonight.' A question mark looming large over the sentence.

'Oh, can I make it for you? I make them every night at the hotel.'

For weeks I had been making prawn cocktails. Shredded lettuce, defrosted prawns (you'd better get three bags out, Nige, we're fully booked tonight), a sauce made from cash-and-carry mayonnaise and tomato ketchup, and then a scattering of chopped parsley and the merest hint of paprika. 'Go easy on the paprika, some of them might not like it. You know what they are like on a Saturday,' chimed Doreen Beckett.

I cut a thin slice from the iceberg lettuce in the fridge. 'I know it doesn't taste of much, but it keeps so well.' I stuff it into two Paris goblets. We only have two. I tear open the prawns, squeeze out the water and drop the pale pink commas into the glasses. We don't have mayonnaise so I shake a glob of salad cream into a Pyrex bowl, then stir in a dollop of tomato ketchup bought specially for the occasion. At the back of the pantry shelf is a tub of Lion brand ground pepper. I shake it into the sauce but the holes are blocked, so prise out the lid with my thumb and pick up a pinch with my fingers. Next to the pepper is a drum of brick-red powder that looks just like the paprika that I use at work. The label says Cayenne but it smells pretty much the same.

My father takes a teaspoon of his prawn cocktail. He glares at me over the top of his glasses. Despite the stern, glassy-eyed look I get the feeling he is about to tell me it is the best prawn cocktail he has ever had in his life. He carries on glaring, his spoon poised mid-air, his eyes suddenly full of tears.

'Is it supposed to be so hot?' Joan asks between sniffs.

'You little bugger,' said my father. A wave of hatred on the last word.

Peach Melba

Sunday lunch at the Talbot was a family affair I slipped into gratefully. Several small tables in the restaurant were pushed together to form one long one, and staff and family sat cheek by jowl, talking about the 'service', the customers, 'I could have killed that old cow on table three,' and the goings-on among the overnight guests, 'I tell you, it's X in room six and that is NOT his wife.' Plates of Diane's beef and pork were passed around the table along with steel dishes of cauliflower cheese and buttered runner beans, and the nattering never stopped.

It was not unusual for the Becketts' two daughters to join us, sometimes with school friends who had turned up for the weekend. They were sweet but always distant, like they belonged to another world. 'Mrs Beckett's son is coming for lunch today,' announced Diane one Sunday morning. 'You haven't seen him yet, have you? He's so good-looking.'

Stuart was indeed good-looking, he also had that air of supreme confidence with the hotel staff that came not just from years at public school but from simply being the owners' son. 'Don't you think he's like David Bowie?' quizzed Di after Stuart and his friend, a short, dark-haired girl with a loud laugh called Beany, walked through the kitchen. I asked if Beany was his girlfriend. 'She could be,' said Diane slowly, making the 'could' last several seconds, then lowered her voice, 'but you know what they say about dancers, don't you?'

I did. And I rather hoped they were right. I wanted to meet, or at least see at close quarters, someone whom my father used to refer to as 'one of them'. Joan called them 'sissies' or on one occasion 'nancy boys' and could reel off their names like the ten times table: Larry Grayson, Kenneth Williams, Frank Ifield, Charles Hawtrey and she 'thought' Frankie Howerd and Bruce Forsyth. 'I'm not sure you're right about old Brucie, you know. I think he's just putting it on,' argued Dad quite rightly. 'Oh and those two boys who sing together,' she would always add, meaning Peter and Gordon. But then Dad and Joan had a bit of thing about people being 'one of them'. Marc Bolan, Michael Crawford, Jimmy Edwards, almost everyone on *Top of the*

Pops was suspected of it and, needless to say, Mick Jagger after he wore a white dress to the open-air concert in Hyde Park. 'Don't be stupid, of course they can't,' snapped my father when I once asked if women could be 'like that too'.

Stuart and Beany ate at the other end of the table amid much hilarity and fooling around. At one point there was even the start of a food fight, though it stopped when old man Beckett walked in to bring more drinks to the table. This was so different from how we ate at home, where even a passing compliment on the food was just 'not done'. At the hotel we always ate up the pies and syllabubs that were left over, but Stuart and Beany went into the kitchen and made vast peach Melbas, leaving a trail of peach juice and drips of strawberry ice cream everyhere. 'They make an exotic couple, like the people you see on the television,' suggested Joyce, one of the cleaners.

'Why don't you go and watch telly with Stuart and his girlfriend?' said Mr Beckett later, as we dried up the wine glasses and filled the shelves in the bar with bottles of Britvic orange and Canada Dry. Doreen suggested exactly the same about ten minutes later and then added, 'You won't be interrupting, she's not his girlfriend, you know, she's just a friend from school.' Doreen Beckett eyeballed me as if she was trying to tell me something.

Stuart and Beany were lying on the bed together, watching a black-and-white film and drinking beers. They certainly looked like girlfriend and boyfriend. 'Come in, my dear,' said Stuart, whose eyelashes suddenly seemed twice as long and black as before. I sat on the floor, my back up against the bed and stared straight at the television. Despite his mother's assurance, I felt almost as much a gooseberry as I did at home.

We sat and watched the film, me listening to every rustle as they rearranged their positions, first his head on her chest, then hers on his, then him lying on his back with Beany's leg underneath him. At one point I felt his knee resting against my neck, and then his leg fell slowly down my side, and he tucked his toes into my elbow; the three of us knotted loosely together like a bowl of spaghetti. I was uncomfortable, yet strangely happy with it.

The film credits rolled up the screen and all of us stirred slightly, stretching our arms and untangling our limbs. Stuart suggested a walk to the river. 'I'm not moving an inch,' said Beany, who was by now almost asleep. 'Come on then, we'll go on our own.' Stuart bounced up and pulled me to my feet.

It was an awkward walk. Long silences, which I didn't know how to fill (I couldn't forget he was my employers' son), accompanied by a sick feeling in my stomach and a desperate need to pee. He was less confident on his own, away from the family and his girlfriend, quiet even. We dawdled along the river bank, as if we were each waiting for something to happen, or to be said. At a patch where the current became stronger, we clambered up through the tall grass and long-stemmed buttercups to a bit of the field

I often came to with Julia. 'Hang on a sec,' I said. 'I've got to pee.'

As I zipped up my jeans Stuart slid his arms round my neck and pulled my face towards him. We kissed briefly, maybe for two or three seconds, then he put his arm round my neck and we ran back to the hotel. 'See you later,' he said and bounced up to his room, two steps at a time. I went into the bar and lay on one of the long, squashy sofas, unsure of what, if anything, had just happened. I had butterflies in my stomach but at the same time felt somehow disappointed. I thought being 'one of them' was going to be much more exciting.

Pickled Walnuts

Once Dad retired he took to picking me up from the school bus in the car. He had traded in his old Rover with its polished leather seats and walnut dash for a new, bright blue Japanese thing that seemed to be made of plastic and smelled of sick. I was embarrassed to be seen in it, and I missed kicking the autumn leaves that gathered in loose piles at the roadside and the buzz I would get from feeling that someone was watching me as I stopped to take piss in the woods.

The greenhouse was Dad's main escape from Joan's do-it-and-dust-it world. The world where nothing mattered more than being seen to be clean and tidy. Warm and damp, the timber-framed greenhouse smelled of potting compost and, faintly, cigarette smoke in spring and the deep herbal notes of green tomatoes in summer. When there was frost on the ground the scent of Dad's orchid collection hung heavy, like you were walking through honey, and passion flowers wound their way along strings above your head. Joan never set foot in the greenhouse, never held a cymbidium to her nose, never snapped a tomato shoot just to sniff it, never picked a single tomato save once, when she caught a stranger helping herself to a pound of Dad's ripest, chasing her off like she was a tomcat protecting its territory. 'These are the ones she's picked,' snapped Joan, holding out a handful of plump, green-shouldered Moneymaker. 'Said she thought it was pick-your-own, I gave her bleedin' pick-your-own.' Dad replied that she should have let her keep them. 'We've got more than enough.'

His face always dropped slightly when he saw what his new wife had produced for supper. 'I don't really know if I can eat all this,' he said meekly one weekday night when he came in from the garden to find melon slices on the table, a roast chicken crackling away in the oven and an apple pie complete with pastry leaves and holly berries resting on the kitchen counter. He seemed afraid to say too much, but it was clear he felt she was going over the top with these midweek meals of three courses, and even, from time to time, a choice of puddings. Then there were the snacks; the little treats she would make him throughout the day and run up to his greenhouse: toasted cheese or

Welsh rarebit, ham sandwiches, slices of strawberry and apple pie or pieces of Battenberg cake. No cup of tea came without its fat slice of Victoria sandwich. I still bought the odd thing home from my school cooking lessons, proud of them as I was, but I had started to pass the results round on the school bus. Four cold rissoles wrapped in tinfoil seemed a somehow pathetic offering now that Joan had taken up making mandarin orange and maraschino cherry pavlova.

Dad had a taste for odd things I didn't understand. A grey-brown ointment called Gentleman's Relish that he used to spread on triangles of toasted Mother's Pride; Campbell's Meatballs in Gravy; Shipphams Chicken Spread sandwiches; Crosse & Blackwell Piccalilli that everyone at school called camel snot; marmalade with whisky in it; porridge with salt instead of sugar; and his precious pickled walnuts – the last sitting in glass jars like anatomical specimens in the damp, dark pantry, tightly sealed against the army of scurrying silverfish that lived under the fridge. 'They're nothing to do with dirt, it's the damp they like,' Joan reminded us every time one made a break for the skirting board. (The silverfish, that is, not the pickled walnuts.)

One weekend when we attended a fête in a field by the river, Dad came back with a jar of pickled walnuts as big as the jars of sherbet lemons that stood behind the sweet counter in the post office. 'It will last us a year or two,' he said, bringing them in from the boot of the car.

'I don't know how you can eat the filthy things,' shuddered Joan, screwing up her nose like he had just handed her a jar of preserved dog poo.

One day I came home to be told that Dad was out playing tennis. The idea of my father without a pipe in his hand was difficult enough, let alone that of him cavorting around on a tennis court. 'Why tennis?' I asked.

'I don't know, your father has just decided he needs to take up some sort of sport now he's retired,' reasoned Joan, though I could tell she wasn't any more convinced than I was. 'It's better than all that funny Masonic business,' she whispered, lowering her voice and making me feel as if for once she was confiding in me. 'He says he's going to be doing it two days a week.'

The Freemasons had always been a big part of Dad's life. He was always out at a lodge meeting, a ladies' night or a charity event. 'It's got something to do with rolling up your trouser leg,' said Joan knowledgeably one night, as if that explained everything. 'It's some sort of code,' she continued, with the implication that millions of professional and apparently sane men travelled hours to roll up their left black trouser leg in front of one another and go home again. The Masons, the greenhouse and now tennis. Why marry her in the first place if he wanted to do so many things that excluded her?

We didn't talk about money, ever. I just suspected that something wasn't right. He had spoken quite crisply to Joan a couple of times recently, once when she bought some smoked salmon to eat before Sunday lunch, and again when she threw a piece of stale cake in the bin. 'There just seem to be so many cakes nowadays?' he said like he was asking a question. Then he quickly added, 'It's just that it could have been a trifle.'

Joan went ballistic. 'Could have been a trifle!' she yelled. 'It could only have been a trifle if I made it into one.' And then: 'Don't you think I've got enough to do? Cleaning up after him, after you, doing the garden, weeding, mowing the lawns, taking the dog out. He doesn't do anything except his homework. Get him to make you a bleedin' trifle.' She tossed her head sideways in my direction. It was like a huge rock had dropped from the sky and just missed us all. My stomach twisted into a knot and I wanted to go to the loo urgently. I just walked out into the garden, avoiding looking at either of them. As I rounded the corner I heard him say, 'I'll get him to do a bit more to help.'

My father came back an hour later with a long-handled lawn trimmer, brand new and obviously expensive. 'It's for doing the edges,' he said apologetically, 'so you don't have to do it on your knees with the little snippers any more.' He must have driven into Bromyard for them. Joan didn't even look up, she just carried on deadheading the roses, a job I knew my father loved dearly, a job he used to do about nine o'clock on a summer's evening after a glass of whisky, but one he never got the chance to do any more. Nowadays his wife did it. One brown edge on a single petal and then even the most exquisite rose suddenly found itself on the compost. A rose bush is much tidier without the roses.

Sweeties

My father had started to look tired and white when he came in from the garden, a faint clamminess to his skin, like wet dough. Things he had always wanted to grow – scented wigwams of sweet peas, rows of broad beans held up with string, soldierly lines of carrots neatly labelled with their varieties – filled every bed, he even grew his own tobacco and dried the long leaves over the bedroom storage heaters. He became obsessed with his orchids, turning one half of the greenhouse into a small rainforest and hanging baskets of miniature variegated orchids from the roof, tiny, like yellow and blood-splattered bees. When he was in a good mood the old man would summon me to look at his latest success, an arching branch of white blossom, edged pink and mauve like the wings of rare butterflies, or a stiff spire of green and maroon buds that had opened to reveal exquisite, explicit blooms.

The new warmth he had given off since his marriage, like a freshly baked loaf, had cooled of late, and he would talk less than he used to. Questions were answered gruffly, or sometimes not at all, and patience, other than with his beloved garden, had worn thin. He took to snapping at me for no particular reason. Fifteen, moodily hormonal and laden with work for my exams, I became an easy target. The air between us became tight and tender, like the skin round an erupting spot.

Once or twice I saw him from the bathroom window clutching at his chest when he was digging the parsnip bed. He would stop, stone still, then rub his chest like he did when he had indigestion. Except that this time he didn't take one of the Setlers he always carried in his trouser pocket. I heard him asking my stepmother why we had to have three courses at every meal now, and why there always had to be a pudding, even on weekdays. One Sunday lunchtime, when we started our roast dinner with soup and finished it with raspberry tart decorated with swirls of buttercream, I remember him saying, 'It's all very nice, Joan, but I really don't need all this.'

When I wasn't working I would spend most of my time in my bedroom, listening to albums – *Madman Across the Water*, *Aladdin Sane*, *Tea for the Tillerman* – in darkness but for the underwater light of the lava lamp. I invented home-work projects too, anything really to get out of having to sit with the newly-weds, a gooseberry in front of the television. 'I don't know what you do in your room all the time,' Joan would moan, accusingly. I am not sure Dad minded what I did, but once she had let her dissatisfaction be known he would be obliged to join in, telling me it wasn't normal for a fifteen-year-old to spend so much time alone in his room. On other occasions she would talk about me as if I wasn't there: 'He's been in his room all afternoon again,' she would say to him, folding her arms tightly across her chest, with me sitting less than six feet away. It wouldn't have mattered if her hostility, so much more open now, hadn't been quite so infectious.

Dad was still a sweetie man, rarely without a Murray Mint, a humbug, a toffee eclair or a Payne's Poppet. There were Toffos in his greenhouse, Liquorice Allsorts in his bedside drawer and a bag of Fox's Glacier Fruits in the glovebox of the car. At weekends he brought in boxes of pastel-coloured fondants or Clarnico Mint Creams, Ruffle bars with their pink coconut filling, and at Christmas liqueur chocolates in amber-, green- and gold-coloured foil. It was then we had crystallised figs too, sticky dates in long boxes, the fruit stuck to the paper lining, and shallow, round packets of sugar-coated orange and lemon slices.

More to my taste were chocolate bars such as Peppermint Aero and Curly Wurlys, the ill-fated Summit bar and Cadbury's sickly Aztec. Dad treated chocolate bars (except for Fruit and Nut and, for some reason, Caramac) as something from a lower order. For him the nadir of sweetie life was a box of chocolate Brazils or the coffee creams in Black Magic.

Sometimes, for no reason at all, he would arrive home with proper boxes of chocolates, Newberry Fruits, Dairy Box or perhaps a long, slender pack of Matchmakers. On special occasions there would be Terry's All Gold. The two of them would tuck in as they sat watching *Des O'Connor*, occasionally, reluctantly, passing the box over to me. 'Did he take two?' Joan would say quietly, no doubt furious that I had nicked the orange cream.

At five foot ten and nine stone it hardly mattered what I ate. 'Hollow legs' was the knee-jerk explanation, though my aunt used to say I had 'worms'. Adrian called me a streak of piss, though not within earshot of Dad. My aunt reckoned my father was the same build as me when he was my age and only started putting on weight at forty. Coming along when he was almost fifty, I had never known him skinny, but one thing was for sure, I had certainly never seen him as big as he was now.

The Two of Us

The school bus pulls up outside the pub and I look out of the window for Dad's blue Japanese thingy. It's there but Dad isn't driving. The car window is rolled down and Joan's son-in-law Martin is sitting at the wheel, his elbow sticking out of the window. He looks like he has a great weight on his mind.

I open the passenger door, throw my satchel in the back and flop into the seat. Flopping was the way you sat down at sixteen. I know, without a word from Martin, that something is wrong. He asks me how I am, what I did at school today. We drive up the hill towards the house, me feeling that I must answer his banal, slightly embarrassed questions calmly and politely because somehow I know there is something terribly, horribly wrong.

As the car pulls up on the drive I can see Joan, walking quickly out to meet me. Her eyes are wet and black and darting left and right, like she's panicking over something. 'I've got something to tell you,' says Martin, in a tone that suggests he has been rehearsing it for the past few hours. He shifts awkwardly in his seat and looks down into his lap. 'Your dad was playing tennis this morning and . . .' Joan gets to the car and pulls the door open and flings her arms round me.

'We are on our own now, son,' she blurts out the words, her voice cracking on the word 'son', and breaks down in tears. I cannot explain why, but I knew, from the second I saw Martin in the car, that Dad was dead. I feel light-headed yet at the same time strangely strong and calm. As my stepmother squeezes me tightly I say nothing (I honestly do not know what to say) and pull away from her, slowly, firmly, though I am careful not to be rude. Martin is out of the car and holding her now. She's sobbing. I take my school bag off the back seat and walk towards the house. I walk in to find a kind, normally rather jolly neighbour talking, grim-faced, on the telephone and his wife, usually so full of laughter, grabs me, hugs me tightly to her and says, to no one in particular, 'Will someone please tell me what I am supposed to say to this boy?'

I walk upstairs, close my bedroom door and sit on my bed. I get the feeling I should be crying. Yet no tears come. There are excited butterflies in my stomach and I can feel something welling up inside me that isn't tears. I feel tingly and warm, like something wonderful is happening. Like I have pins and needles in my limbs. I bite my bottom lip hard, not to stop the tears, but to check that this is really happening.

Another Funeral

The flowers were lovely, as you could only hope for a man for whom the joys of gardening were on a par with that of sexual intercourse. The weather had been kind, the onlookers from the village respectful and the vicar as generous as he could be about someone he had known only as a corpse.

As funerals went it was unexpectedly beautiful, romantic even, in a little church nestled at the bottom of the hill, the sun streaming on to the coffin through stained-glass windows. The coffin was walnut like Dad's pipe and had heavy brass handles, the hearse as shiny and black as Dad's Brylcreemed hair had been to the day he died. It all went quite well really, at least until the hearse swung slowly past us. You could almost hear the family's collective intake of breath as they spotted the discreet sign 'Co-operative Funeral Service' next to the coffin. Everyone knew Dad would rather have been put out for the dustmen than be buried by the Co-op.

The burial was in a pretty, hillside graveyard in a village called Suckley, a place he had been to only once before, when we got lost on the way to Hereford. I was extremely happy with the venue Joan chose, with its cascading dog roses and lichen-covered gravestones, but there were grumbles from other quarters. His sister wanted him to be put to rest next to their mother in a niche off the Walsall Road in Birmingham, though some might say that no one could possibly rest in a niche just off the Walsall Road in Birmingham. Then someone pointed out that they had never got on terribly well, so it seemed a little unkind to lump them together now, just for the sake of tidiness.

The congregation's rendition of 'The Lord is my Shepherd' made me cry, as did the splendid array of bobbing white lilies on the coffin. The emotions were no more than I would get on any occasion where organ music was involved. To be honest I'd have burst into tears if someone played the Hokey Cokey on a church organ.

Joan fussed over me all week, making steak for my tea and calling me 'son'. A sign, some said cruelly, that Dad's will had yet to be read. But then she needn't have worried, for, as anyone knows, there is nothing that quite turns an old man's attention in your direction like an offer of sex and home-made cake.

Apple Pie and a Wake-up Call

'Right, make five apple pies,' said Jim, his sour, beery breath coming as a shock so early in the morning. No mention of a recipe, or where to find the flour, the butter, the apples, the sugar or even where the tap was for the water. I almost walked out then and there, red-faced and panicking.

The Sun Hotel was a rather typical three-star county town hotel, with net curtains that had seen better days and a dining room that smelled like the duster bag on a Hoover. The carpets were tired green wool with pink and gold rococo swirls and the chairs dark blue leatherette. It was the tables that you noticed, though, crisp white cloths starched to snapping point, shining silver cutlery and glass jugs of iced water. There were butter pats on tiny silver dishes filled with ice, immaculate napkins that crackled when you unfolded them and typewritten menus which were slotted into blue leatherette menu holders to match the chairs.

The menu was typical of any other county hotel that thought enough of itself to banish men without a tie, and women would not be permitted to dine in trousers. Anyone unsuitably attired could eat in the 'buttery': melon 'au porto', consommé, pâté maison, choice of fruit juices, or hors d'œuvres from the trolley. And then the main courses: fillets of sole Véronique, deep-fried haddock or plaice with tartare sauce, gammon and pineapple, roast lamb and mint sauce. Plus the standard note at the bottom that all main courses are served with 'vegetables of the day'. The à la carte menu, a vast list of dishes Escoffier might have recognised but which now came from a tin, rarely saw light of day.

This was hardly a job for life, just a way to earn more money than the Talbot could offer before catering college started in the autumn, a way to escape the packing up of the house, the giving away of the plants from Dad's greenhouse and hearing Joan refer to everything as hers instead of ours.

Stiff with panic, I tried to remember the recipe for sweet shortcrust pastry. I couldn't even remember the ingredients, let alone the ratio of butter to flour. It didn't help that I had never made an apple pie in my life. 'Stores are along the corridor, you'll find pie dishes in the wash-up,' snapped Jim, slapping his beer belly like he was proud of it. 'And get a fuckin' move on, you've the hors d'œuvre trolley to do yet.' Head down, I marched along to the storeroom to find, thankfully, several open sacks of flour.

I weighed the flour and cut up the margarine I found in the walk-in fridge into chunks the size of dice. I tipped the whole lot into a big aluminium bowl I found on the slatted shelf under the table and started to rub the butter into the flour with my fingertips, like we had at school, like Joan had, like Diane had. 'Use the Hobart, we'll be all fuckin' day else,' choked Jim, returning from the storeroom, wiping his mouth with the back of his hand.

It was only by chance I clocked the word Hobart, a label attached to a giant version of a Kenwood Chef, the machine caked in congealed food and badly leaking oil. 'Oh, give it here,' he pounced, snatching the bowl out of my hand and tipping the flour and butter into the grubby bowl of the

Hobart. He turned it on from a switch so covered in flyblow you didn't know what colour it was. Flour shot out at all angles. He threw a cup of water in and kept turning the beater till it was mixed. 'Now, roll that out and line the bottom of them dishes.'

The apples, now peeled and cut into thick slices, Jim told me to put on to boil with a few spoonfuls of water and some sugar. I stood watching the yellow fruit intently, not wanting to catch the eye of two other chefs, Frank, a grey-haired man in his fifties who had no teeth and shuffled and held on to things like he was losing his balance, and Tony, who spoke with an Irish accent so strong I couldn't understand a word he said. Suddenly Jim squatted down and picked up a tired apple pie from the bottom tier of the wooden sweet trolley. He brought it over to the simmering apples and crumbled the whole thing, pastry and fruit into the simmering apples. He turned away without a word.

At lunchtimes the revolving hors d'œuvre trolley was wheeled around the tables, offering diners a choice of cucumber in vinegar, thinly sliced tomatoes with chopped chives on top, egg mayonnaise with a cross of anchovy fillets and capers, a dusting of paprika on each egg. There was Russian salad – diced carrot, potato, onions and peas in a snow-white mayonnaise – sliced beetroot in vinegar and rollmop herrings. You could have as much or as little as you wanted, which was probably its only appeal. The grated carrot salad was fresh enough.

Frank walked like his shoes belonged to a bigger man.

The backs of his shoes were squashed flat, the edges frayed, and his fat belly only drew attention to his filthy apron. He smelled more than slightly of pee. 'Has he done the fish yet?' Frank asked of no one in particular, jerking his head in my direction. 'Doing the fish' turned out to be a weekly job of washing the batter off fillets of haddock and plaice under the tap in the still room then rebattering them with new stuff. 'It's the batter that goes off, not the fish, isn't it, Jim?'

Just before twelve-thirty the waitresses came into the kitchen, all black dresses and little white aprons, and stood in a gaggle, gossiping around the hotplate. 'Come on, girls, get your tits out,' said Frank as he started putting battered silver dishes of vegetables in the hot cupboard. He grabbed the thigh of a blonde waitress, mid-twenties, hair in a bun. 'Cor, I'd like to fuck you, darlin',' Frank said as he ran his hand up her skirt. Unfazed, she pushed him off without a word, like nothing more than a fly that had landed on her.

Jim sat at a small table by the deep-freeze, a half-drunk pint by his elbow. 'Right, ladies, don't forget to bring in all your dirty panties tomorrow. I need them to make the fish stock,' he announced. Dipping hunks of bread into cups of tomato soup, none of the waitresses missed a beat of their conversation. It was as if he hadn't spoken. Jim looked pleased with himself like he'd just said the funniest thing ever. I smiled weakly at him. It wasn't so much what he said that was disgusting. It was the lecherous way the unshaven, greasy-haired beer-breath had said the word 'panties'.

'Two soup of day, two fried fish, Jim,' announced Molly, a waitress so old and bent her eyes looked permanently down at the floor.

'Frank . . . Frank . . . there's an order in,' yelled Jim, who didn't budge from his seat.

'He's gone for a shite,' muttered back Tony. The only words I had heard him say that I could understand. 'More like he's gone for a fucking wank.'

Frank shuffled back into the kitchen, wiping his hands on his encrusted apron. He snatched two pieces of newly rebattered fish and dropped them into the deep-fat fryer, then two handfuls of pre-cooked chips into another. 'Ask the old cow if they're havin' any veg, will you?' Frank asked a young waitress with blue eyeshadow, then followed on, 'I bet you were shaggin' again last night, weren't you, you filthy little bitch?'

She smiled back, mock warmly, the corner of her lip curling into a snarl. 'Yeah, in your dreams, Frank sweetie, in your fucking dreams.'

I hung around waiting for someone to order pâté maison, grapefruit, scampi tartare or anything off what Jim called the 'ally cart' menu. No one did, so I grabbed a cloth and started wiping some of the tea stains and flyblow off the work surfaces. 'What are you, a fuckin poof?' snapped Jim. 'Go and get some fresh rolls, they're running out. And stop cleaning like a woman.' Fresh rolls turned out to be yesterday's that were dunked in a sink of cold water then rebaked in a very hot oven.

Tony and Jim both disappeared at different points during 'service'. I suspected they had snuck off to the pub till Tony announced something about 'havin' the squits'.

The staff toilets were down a short corridor at the rear of the kitchen on the way to the bins. The floor was dotted with cockroaches that someone seemed to have stamped on. The stench of stale pee was enough to make your eyes water. In the week I stuck it out at the Sun Hotel the solitary bar of green soap in the men's toilets remained untouched, as dry and cracked as the batter on my rebattered fish.

A Sniff of Basil

We made sauce mornay endlessly at catering college, as we did glossy-brown sauce Espagnole, demi-glace and bland, floury sauce béchamel. We made potatoes into little balls – 'Parisienne' they called it; we turned carrots and potatoes into six-sided barrels then made pommes duchesse with the trimmings. College was obsessed with classical French cooking, especially the 'mother' sauces and their variations and garnishes, the details of which we had to know by heart like the nine times table. Why we couldn't just look up the correct accompaniment for a serving of caviar in a book was beyond me. All that mattered to them was that we knew how to garnish caviar with finely chopped egg yolk, finely chopped egg white, finely chopped onion, finely chopped parsley. None of us had even seen real caviar. More to the point, most us never would.

If we made a flour and butter 'roux' once we made it a thousand times. By the end of our first term most of us could make sauce mornay in our sleep. We could also have rattled off a sea of sauce Véronique too, which was a pity because there hadn't been much call for fish in white sauce with skinned grapes since 1935. Going through the entire repertoire of fancy-schmancy classical French cooking was one thing, the total refusal of the college chefs to acknowledge French bourgeois cooking was another.

I wanted to learn, no, to *eat* moules marinière, boeuf bourguignon, cassoulet, confit de canard, salade Niçoise, pissaladière, coq au vin, Saint Émilion au chocolat. Instead, we made sauce mornay, and béchamel and Véronique and Espagnole, and learned every garnish in *Larousse*. I left catering college with an unsurpassable knowledge of French classical cookery. The fact I didn't know how to roast a chicken, grill a steak, make a chocolate mousse or even make a decent green salad was quite irrelevant. What was even worse was that it took me twenty years to learn that caviar is infinitely better with nothing but lemon and crisp, lightly buttered toast.

Yet there was someone who understood. Joe Yates worked only part-time at the college, taking an afternoon class called, somewhat cringingly, Continental Cookery. Joe was sixty and he looked it: round-faced, his skin was creased from years of standing over a hot stove at his family restaurant a few miles away. Joe swore, to the amusement of the girls in the class. Not just the occasional bugger or sod but fuck and shit and bollocks and balls, which got a chorus of giggles every time. He told us endless jokes, rude rather than dirty, and once told us that he refused to give Elizabeth David one of his recipes because the last time he wrote out a recipe for her the doyenne of food writers had failed to credit him. (In her later books she became scrupulous about such matters.) He used a different language from the other chefs who, in fairness, had to stick to a strict and hopelessly outdated syllabus.

Joe talked of lasagne, of gnocchi, fettucine and saltimbocca. He cooked with fresh basil and bay and fennel and mint, he used olive oil instead of butter, and garlic that was plump and white not wizened and beige. Unlike the other chefs he let us taste the food we made, not just from a teaspoon 'to check the seasoning' but by the forkful, everyone standing around and tucking in. His cooking smelled different: aromatic, enticing, almost heady and, as I said, we were allowed to eat it.

One afternoon we turned up to class to be told that Mr Yates had suffered a heart attack that morning and wouldn't be returning. It was like someone had opened a door in a long, dark wall, a door that had let in a shaft of brilliant sunlight. Then they had slammed it shut.

Irish Stew

For those students who didn't live near to college there was help in finding somewhere to stay. You were interviewed briefly by a welfare officer, who would look at you through squinting eyes then match you to a suitable family, insisting that 'They are just the sort of people you need, I'm sure you'll fit in.' Rent was paid either by your parents, a council grant, or in my case, by taking a part-time job. I was sent to live with Mr and Mrs Pearman, a surly, retired geography teacher and his devoutly Christian wife, who lived in a rambling, slightly shambolic pink house on the outskirts of the city. I loved them from the second I clapped eyes on them.

Mrs Pearman was the sort of warm, large-chested woman you wanted to hug but never quite did. She did the church flowers and ran the Brownies, and made pudding with every meal. Anything you did that she disapproved of – swearing, being late for meals, forgetting your key, farting ('I HEARD that!' she would bellow) – was brought up at breakfast, starting with 'Dad says . . .' She put me in an attic room, once occupied by her sons, with a student called Bruce, one year my senior. The two of us fought from day one.

Mrs Pearman's house was a home in every sense of the word. A place where a daughter or son would suddenly turn up without warning, expecting, and getting, supper or Sunday lunch. Where every piece of furniture seemed to have a history and where every family event was faithfully recorded in photograph albums. It was warm and happy, untidy and cosy. There was always a jug of garden flowers on the kitchen table and milk in the fridge. And like all good homes Mrs Pearman's also had an overriding smell of golden retriever.

Like the dedicated Brown Owl that she was, Mrs P. cooked everything in her pressure cooker. Not just winter soups and stews and bean hotpots, but EVERYTHING. If she could have washed her drawers in it she would have. 'It's because you cook everything together and only use one gas ring' was her perfectly reasonable excuse, but I did wonder if it was simply that she got a buzz out of cooking in a tightly corked pot that threatened to explode at any moment.

No matter what aficionados may tell you, the downside of a pressure cooker is that everything that comes out of one tastes the same. There is a pressure-cooked 'flavour' that permeates every onion, swede, haricot bean and lump of meat, every jam sponge and rice pudding. I grew to love Mrs P.'s pressure cooking as much as I loved her chaotic, warm and comfy home. Her vegetable soup for Saturday lunch; her Tuesday liver and mash; the Wednesday steamed syrup sponge and the Sunday boiled gammon and mashed parsnip. I loved her morning coffee and her night-time cocoa, her Monday salads with their steamed potatoes (even with their little black eyes) and, above all, her gorgeous Friday hotpot. But there is no getting away from the fact that whatever you cook in a pressure cooker it always, always tastes of Irish stew.

Black Forest Gâteau

Getting a holiday job between college terms meant the difference between Saturday shopping at Oxfam (threadbare Crombies, brown nylon slacks with dodgy yellow stains on the insides of the pockets) and shopping at Number One, Worcester's only men's 'boutique' (tear-drop collar shirts and velvet jackets). Frankly, there wasn't much else to do in Worcester on a Saturday afternoon. Number One was rumoured to have a two-way mirror in the changing room so that the owner, a rather exotic Marc Bolan look-alike, known fondly as Pete the Poof, could watch his customers trying on their jeans. Everyone knew he always gave you a size too small so that he could watch you squeezing your packet into them.

I got a job at a grand hotel just outside the city. We had all trooped round it on a college day out and I knew at once it would be a world away from the Sun. With all its velvet drapes and little gold banqueting chairs, the hotel had the sort of glamour I had previously only seen in brochures and magazines. My first day there was at the time of an unimaginably over-the-top wedding, where the bride and groom arrived by horse-drawn coach like a scene from

Cinderella, the horses complete with fluffy white plumes on their manes. I was right: nothing could be further from my week at the Sun, especially when the bride came round after lunch with sugared almonds for every member of staff. Even then, nothing could quite top the excitement of knowing that Noel Gordon had been there that afternoon, filming an episode of *Crossroads*.

I had never held a silver salver with twenty portions of tournedos Rossini on it before, let alone one with a border of pommes duchesse and tomatoes stuffed with peas. Standard Midlands wedding breakfast it may have been but it was as near as I had ever been to that sort of food. This was silver service, where the waitresses walked round the room with hot salvers of food on their arm, then deposited it on the guests' plates with the help of a large spoon and fork. I coped with the first course, a sort of prawn cocktail with brandy in the dressing served in Paris goblets, and by the time the main dish had been served I knew that spoon and forkery was for me. What is more, I just loved putting a plate of food in front of someone.

Dessert was a series of giant baked Alaskas studded with sparklers which were lit just as the lights in the dining room were dimmed. Twenty-two waitresses and I trooped out in a fizzing, spluttering daisy chain to the strains of the 'Sugar Plum Fairy', and made our way through the maze of long tables lit only by the light from the fireworks that cascaded from our giant puddings. 'I can smell my uniform singeing,' hissed one of the old ducks, who obviously felt that this act of pyrotechnics was beyond the call of wait-ressing duty. 'I'm going to demand danger money next week. I don't know why they can't just have cheese and biscuits.'

The waitresses loved having a lanky, spotty male, who wore his hormones on his sleeve, in their midst. The chefs, who uniformly wore stubble and oversized clogs and all looked like they washed their hair once a year, couldn't understand why a guy would want to 'waitress' instead of cook. From day one they called me darlin'.

Banqueting food was somewhat predictable fare, a rota of the aforementioned tournedos Rossini, duck à l'orange or Montmorency, chicken Kiev, rack of lamb (accompanied without fail by tomatoes stuffed with peas, carrots and sweetcorn), beef Wellington and in summer cold salmon. Vegetables were invariably petits pois à la Française, and desserts (we never called them puddings) were pavlova, charlotte russe, trifle, chocolate soufflé (the mousse version that was set with gelatine, rather than the oven job) and the most popular, Black Forest gâteau.

Starters were prawn cocktail and soup, which was invariably watercress. For some reason watercress was con-sidered posh. Nine out of ten weddings involved prawn cocktail, beef wellington and Black Forest gâteau, which for some reason we called Gâteau Forêt-Noire. Or gatta-forrey-nwwarrr, as the waitresses referred to it in thick Midlands accents. I used to pray that someone would decline their squidgy cake, so I could wolf the cold chocolate sponge, the super-white whipped cream and the chocolate flakes that covered the sides – chocolate sprinkles were considered a bit downmarket – but very few ever did. In Midlands eating-out circles, ending your meal with a slice of chocolate gâteau was a point of honour. Staff food was taken in a canteen thick with cigarette smoke, an unending round of chicken and chips, followed by whatever was left from the various dessert trolleys.

I suppose I was taken in by the apparent luxury of it all: the velvet drapes, the vast high-backed sofas and the potted palms. A bit of red velvet goes a long way to a boy brought up with G-Plan. After a week or so I started to spot the flies in the ointment. An ancient chef the size of a toby jug who used white bread in the trifle because he couldn't be bothered to make sponge. 'Bah, they'll never know and if they do they'd be too embarrassed to say.' The wine waiters who 'miscounted' the number of bottles of champagne sold at weddings and who could later be seen humping crates of it over to staff quarters. The waitresses who filled empty bottles of Malvern water from the cold tap before a 'function' and the platters of smoked salmon tea sandwiches that were padded out with finely grated carrot. I'd seen filthy food before but this was something new, a world where customers are treated as being stupid enough not know the difference between salmon and carrot. This was also the first time I had witnessed food prepared in such quantity (prawn cocktail for two hundred wasn't unusual) or worked with chefs who all seemed barely old enough to drive. This was also the first time I'd been in a situation where sex was as much on tap as Watney's Red Barrel.

To say there was an atmosphere of promiscuity at the hotel was like saying they make a bit of cheese in Roquefort. Sex oozed from every brick in the hotel's walls. The staff quarters, a good hundred yards from the hotel, was planet party, a place where the strains of Pink Floyd and *Madman Across the Water* were to be heard twenty-four/seven and where you were more likely to get a dose of the clap than a decent night's kip. It would have been almost impossible not to get laid. I was put into a small two-bed room with a blond, baby-faced wine waiter called Tim, who seemed to possess nothing more than three wine books, a bottle of Fabergé Brut and a single pair of socks. After a supper that consisted of three slices of stolen Black Forest gâteau and a bottle of Schweppes bitter lemon, I snuggled down to sleep, only to spend the rest of the night awake while Tim humped a particularly sweet, mild-mannered waitress like he was trying to get into *The Guinness Book of Records*.

Seafood Cocktail

By now the prawn cocktail's glitzy image was beginning to tarnish, even in the Midlands. Every restaurant, even the local pub, had it on its menu, just above the trout with almonds. Some tried serving it in a tall-stemmed hock glass, others in a champagne saucer. People ordered prawn cocktail because they thought it was posh, and restaurants loved it because it was a money spinner. But it had worked its way downhill and its time had come.

In an elaborate attempt to prolong its popularity, and therefore their profit, some smart restaurateurs got the idea of the seafood cocktail. This had the obligatory prawns but also the new luxury of squid and bottled mussels. The lettuce and Marie Rose sauce remained, but the addition of a miniature rose made from tomato skin wound round and round in the form of a rosette and perched next to the parsley sprig was all new. It was prawn cocktail all dressed up for a ball. Or in this case a dinner-dance.

Every Saturday there would be at least two 'functions', usually weddings, and during the week a number of conferences to be catered for. This was mass catering, but with knobs on. The tables were laid with glittering silver, the flowers a match for Chelsea and the little red velvet and gilt chairs made even the fattest of guests feel elegant. But after only a week I could see through it.

Tim had forbidden me to tell anyone who he was shagging. 'Tell anyone and I'll kill you,' he threatened. Nice guy. The simple truth was that she had a boyfriend who was a mate of all the other chefs, who she would go back to at the end of her summer job at the hotel. But for the time being she would spend most nights with Tim. Everyone knew they were friends, even that she stayed in our room, but no one guessed they were sleeping together.

One lunchtime I had been sent to the kitchen to help out because they were short-staffed. Six of us were making seafood cocktail for the biggest wedding we had ever catered for. Huge washing-up bowls held defrosted prawns, long white sacks and rings of squid, and bottled mussels, rinsed of their vinegar. I had made the secret sauce. Which as anyone who has ever been within twenty feet of the catering industry knows is nothing more than salad cream, tomato ketchup, Worcestershire sauce and Tabasco. I was busy stirring a gallon of sauce into the rings of squid and little pink prawns when Martin, one of the grubby bunch of chefs, asked if he could borrow my melon-baller. 'I didn't bring it down, it's in my room. If you want it you'll have to go and get it,' I said, literally up to my elbows in Marie Rose sauce.

He returned from our room with the melon-baller looking smug. Or at any rate smugger than usual. 'Who's Tim shagging then?' he said.

'No one,' I snapped, remembering my room-mate's threat.

'So whose is this then?' he said, swinging a used condom round in his hand, stretching it – somewhat dangerously I thought – like a catapult.

'Dunno,' I lied. I made a grab at the condom. The chef threw it over to one of the others, I jumped up for it. Missed again. They continued throwing the condom back and forth while I made pathetic attempts at snatching it back, like a puppy being teased with a ball. The last time I looked the condom was sailing through the air above the bowls of cocktail de crevettes, sauce Marie Rose.

'Where's that fucking seafood salad?' yelled the head chef as he marched in, the head waiter hot on his tail and two hundred bib-and-tuckered wedding guests waiting for their starter. 'Yes, chef. Ready, chef. Yes, chef,' we chorused. Within seconds champagne glasses were filled with shredded lettuce, prawns, squid and vinegary mussels, garnished with the obligatory rose and the sprig of parsley, and out they went to the wedding party by the hundred.

The guests munched politely. 'Who's got Tim's rubber then?' said Martin. There was a silence, followed by a short argument about who had it last. Martin admitted throwing it in the air just as chef had walked in, yet no one seemed to have caught it. No one had seen it land. We checked the floor, the table. We all stood there, just staring at the empty bowls that had held the seafood salad. Someone sniggered.

'I want to see every glass and plate that comes back,' yelled Martin as we all ran to the wash-up in time to catch the first of the waitresses bringing back a tray of dirty crockery. But with the exception of the odd stray tomato rose and unwanted sprig of parsley every glass was scraped clean. Every plate returned empty. Every last prawn, mussel and ring of squid had been eaten.

La Steak Diane

The jewel in the hotel's crown was Aphrodite's, a small, formal French restaurant 'done out' in deep purple and gold. For those of us who worked in the banqueting rooms or the cut and come-again carvery, Aphrodite's remained something of a mystery. The small tables were set with silver that glistened in the candlelight, and the waiters – dark, exclusively French or Italian and impossibly cute – moved around the tables with that easy professionalism that can spot a woman about to leave the table or a cigarette that needs lighting seconds before it happens. The place ran like a well-oiled engine. None of us from the plebeian quarters of banqueting were allowed to so much as peep behind its velvet-curtained entrance.

I longed to taste the food whose scents wafted through when Aphrodite's purple curtain swooshed open to permit a guest to enter or leave. The smells were the results of the chemistry you get when you mix brandy, shallots, cream and French cooks together with the fumes from a metholated spirit lamp. This magical whiff was the result of the then fashionable habit of cooking food in front of the guests, in a shallow copper pan over a silver spirit lamp set on a side table.

The most exalted of all lamp cookery was the making of steak Diane – batted-out slices of beef, fried with butter, finely chopped shallots, brandy, stock, smooth mustard, lemon juice, Worcestershire sauce and, invariably, though quite incorrectly, cream. The smell from the spirit stove as the chopped shallots were being softened in the melted butter was one that is for ever imprinted on the memory of anyone who has ever been to such a restaurant. Once the brandy had ignited (a trick which never failed to impress the gin, tonic and peroxide crowd) the steak was plated, the sauce poured over and the dish put in front of the customer while the food was still sizzling.

This was show-off cooking of the highest order. Its point was to be as rich, flamboyant and alcoholic as possible. The average meal went something like this: a round of gin and tonics in the lounge bar, followed by a bottle of Asti Spumante with the first course – usually crab bisque or prawn cocktail; a bottle of Mouton Cadet with the steak Diane; and then crêpes Suzette – an equally alcohol-laden recipe of pancakes flashed at the table in brandy, orange and lemon juice and marmalade – hotly followed by brandies warmed over the spirit stoves. God alone knows how anyone got home.

I so wanted to taste that steak Diane. I could have made it myself in the staff kitchen but it wouldn't have been the same; the chichi splendour of Aphrodite's seemed an essential seasoning. In a somewhat desperate attempt I booked a table under an anonymous name for me and a sweet, doe-eyed waitress called Linda, who for some reason had become besotted with me. She had already proved herself to be up for pretty much anything. The waiters in

Aphrodite's seemed from another, distant world and were unlikely to recognise a couple of staff from the banqueting rooms. We turned up in our best clothes – she looked fabulous in navy-blue and white Laura Ashley, a black Alice band in her hair and enough make-up to qualify for the job of Buttons in a provincial production of *Cinderella*. I was less convincing, though I had shaved off the pathetic tufts of bumfluff that sprouted from my chin and of which I was strangely proud; I even went so far as to buy a new shirt specially for the occasion. I also doused myself in enough Eau Sauvage to bring tears to the eyes of anyone within six feet.

We walked briskly, heads down, through the hotel lobby and down the thick red stair carpet to the restaurant bar, trails of Christian Dior following close behind. We took our table, a tiny one slap bang in the middle of the room, where we were handed menus the size of Switzerland. Barely bothering to look at the display of dishes I ordered confidently for both of us, like I had done it a thousand times before. 'We'll start with the seafood pancake and a crab bisque, then we'll both have the steak tartare with creamed spinach and pommes allumettes. Oh, and a bottle of Beaujolais Villages, thank you.' I couldn't wait.

The seafood pancake was rich but quite the most delicious thing I had ever tasted. Tiny prawns and juicy mussels wrapped up in a soft pancake, the creamy sauce slowly oozing out as I cut through the crêpe. Once our plates were cleared the waiter, who was, to be honest, being a bit over-friendly with my girlfriend, pulled up his little side table. Another waiter brought several dishes on a white-clothed tray and laid them down one by one.

I am not sure exactly when I realised I had ordered steak tartare instead of steak Diane. I remember believing that the raw minced beef, the raw egg yolks and the Tabasco sauce would somehow manage to become my longed-for steak Diane right up to the moment the waiter proudly put the results in front of me. I looked down at the plate of raw, pink mince with the two perfect golden egg yolks in the middle, like birds in a nest. I suddenly realised that I could hear every voice in the room, even whispered conversations several tables away, loud and clear, yet I couldn't hear a single word my girlfriend was saying. I felt cold, then hot, then cold again. The little egg yolks seemed to be looking up at me, laughing. Then everyone was laughing. My father's face flashed across my plate, laughing. Little beads of sweat began to appear on my brow. My head started to swim. I felt as if I was drowning in a cocktail of Christian Dior and the fumes from the spirit stove on the next table. 'Are you all right, you've gone all white?' said Linda.

The next thing I knew I was lying outside on the marble steps of the hotel, slowly coming round in the warm summer air, feeling white, cold, shaky and sticky.

To this day I have never managed to taste steak Diane.

Cold Roast Beef

The chefs at the hotel were all in their twenties, though some of them acted considerably younger. For many of us – and for me – it was the first time away from the watchful, hopeful eyes of our parents, which allowed us to drink, smoke and shag at will. The flip side of the coin was that we never had any clean socks or pants. It also meant we grew our hair longer than was perhaps wise. At one point mine touched my shoulders, fine when it was a bit greasy and stuck to my head, but bad news after a wash when I suddenly had more hair than Farrah Fawcett-Majors.

No one ever really dated at the hotel. You never managed to go out for a drink or to see a movie. You just worked all day, slept in the two hours you got off between clearing away lunch and setting up for dinner, then met up in bed at night. Every night. On your days off you just slept (and slept, and slept), tucked up under the sheets, trying to get over the previous seventy-two hours' work and six sleep-less nights.

If the hours sound grim let me tell you that life itself was anything but. It is truly amazing just how much you can put up with when you are getting regular sex. Seventy-two hours a week is fine so long as it is punctuated with copious quantities of hot, sticky summer-nights' shagging. That, I now know, is why so many hotels have live-in accommodation. It's the only way they can get any staff. 'Accommodation available' after a job advertisement is the proprietor's way of letting prospective staff know that no matter how isolated the hotel they will still get laid.

The problem with having quite so much sex is that, like ice cream, you just want more and more. There is never a point at which you say, OK, enough's enough. One night, just before I went to my room, I slipped up the back stairs to the empty banqueting kitchen to sneak some supper. I had pinched a couple of soft bread baps from the carvery kitchen and fancied a sandwich with some of the rare roast beef I had seen them slicing and laying out on silver trays for the next day's conference. I thought nothing of the cold-room door being open, such sloppiness was hardly unusual among the trainee chefs. There, in front of the silver trays of cold roast beef was Terry, one of the sweeter young chefs, his back towards me. He glanced fleetingly over his shoulder, a coy, schoolboy-style grin slowly widening from ear to ear. Terry was just popping his cork into a slice of soft, rose-pink roast beef.

The Wimpy Bar

I get a phone call from my brother. He says that Joan has sold up and moved back to the Midlands, and she is suggesting that I move in with her. Quite where she thinks I will work in her neck of the woods is a mystery, and Adrian cracks a joke about me getting a job at the Wimpy Bar. I don't like to point out that a girlfriend and I have just been banned from the one in Worcester after a drunken binge that ended up with her throwing up over her Coca-Cola float. I point out that they may not even have a Wimpy in Wolverhampton.

I have no idea why Joan should want me on the scene again, assuming that she has, like me, said good riddance. I can only assume that the hoped-for reunion with her family hasn't happened or has not turned out to be quite the picnic she would have wished. I am not sure why, but the thought makes me sink into a black hole. I know how much she was looking forward to meeting up with her two estranged daughters again, and indeed, just after Dad died, there had been a flurry of letters and Barbara, the eldest, had made brief contact. Joan would be distraught if this didn't work. Perhaps you can't just walk in ten years later and say 'your dinner is on the table' as if nothing had happened.

I get a handful of coins from the bar and go to the telephone box in the staff quarters. I stand there for a full three or four minutes waiting impatiently behind a Spanish waiter, who is jabbering away at the top of his voice, the coins getting sweaty in my hand. I am honestly not sure what I am going to say, I guess I just want to know she is all right. Then suddenly, as the waiter punches another coin into the slot, I turn and walk away.

Pommes Dauphinoise

When my father was alive our eating out had been confined to the Berni Inn in Hereford. We usually skipped starters (I think we once had the honeydew melon but Joan said it wasn't ripe) and went straight to steak, fat ones that came on an oval plate with grilled tomatoes, onion rings, fried mushrooms and wonderful, fat golden chips. We drank lemonade and lime except for Joan who had a Tio Pepe, and then had ice cream for afters. Sometimes my aunt would take me to the Gay Tray in Rackham's store in Birmingham where we would queue up with our gay trays and choose something hot from the counter, poached egg on toast for her, Welsh rarebit and chips for me. There had been the odd afternoon tea taken in seaside hotels (two-toasted-teacakes-and-a-pot-of-tea-for-two, please) and tea taken at garden centres (four-coffees-with-cream-and-four-slices-of-coffee-cake, if you would) and, once, a memorable tea eaten in Devon with slices of home-made ginger cake, scones, cream and little saucers of raspberry jam. But that was it really. Eating out was something other people did.

My last year at catering college I met Andy Parffrey (boxer's nose, public school, played rugby at weekends). He had a stunningly beautiful girlfriend called Lorella. 'You can't possibly marry,' I pleaded one lunchtime over too much lager in the college pub. 'Lorella Parffrey sounds like something you'd eat with a long-handled teaspoon.'

Andy was no more impressed with our syllabus of œuf mayonnaise, sole véronique and sauce Espagnole than I was. We sat together, cooked together, cribbed together. We even took an evening job together at a gentle Queen Anne country house where they served cheese soup, veal cutlet and 'desserts from the trolley'. But Andy knew about things I had never even dreamed of: restaurants where they baked salmon in pastry with currants and ginger, where pork was grilled and topped with melted Gruyère, and where they brought brick-red fish soup to the table with toasted croutes, grated cheese and rust-coloured rouille. He spoke of restaurants with names from another world: the Horn of Plenty and the Hole in the Wall, the Wife of Bath and The Carved Angel.

While Andy and I spent our weekdays together, his weekends and evenings were reserved strictly for Lorella. It took weeks of persuading to get him to go out for dinner, but when he did it became a regular thing. We clocked up visits to several of the better known local restaurants, and would often drive for an hour or more to get to some place on which *The Good Food Guide* had bestowed its prestigious 'pestle and mortar'. Each meal was a gorgeous discovery: tongue with a verdant green sauce; crab tart with buttery pastry; fish soup brought to the table in a white china tureen; quenelles of pike as big as meringues; rabbit with bacon and mustard sauce. We had main dishes that reeked of garlic and basil and rosemary and lemon. Puddings flavoured with coffee and bitter chocolate, almonds and elderflowers. I had never imagined food like this, presented on simple white plates without tomatoes stuffed with peas or piped turrets of potato or roses made from tomato skins. This was food that was made simply to be enjoyed rather than to impress.

Thornbury Castle was surrounded by softly striped lawns and rows of Müller-Thurgau vines. As we drove through the arched gateway, we saw a woman approaching the back door with a wicker basket piled high with field mushrooms, and a young girl in jeans and a striped butcher's apron sprinting back from the walled garden with a handful of dill fronds. Walking towards the front door, me in a rather dodgy sage-green jacket, Andy in blue pinstripe and a tie with a knot as big as my fist, we caught the faintest scent of garlic coming from the open kitchen window. The summer air was still and warm and dense, heavy with garlic, mown grass, lavender, tarragon, framboise and sudden wafts of aniseed.

White wine came in tall glasses with long, thin stems, tiny beads of condensation frosting the outside; little anchovy puffs arrived fresh from the oven with a dish of fat olives the colour of a bruise. We sat on chairs at either side of the fireplace, admiring the tapestries, the jugs of lilies and the polished panelling. The handwritten menu offered familiar things: chicken liver pâté and onion soup, but also things that were new to me: chicken baked with

Pernod and cream, salmon with dill sauce, and lamb with rosemary and apricots. I chose chicken with tarragon sauce. Andy had the veal paupiette, which arrived the size of a Cornish pasty and with a dark, sticky sauce flecked with matchsticks of tongue, parsley and gherkins. The food was like that Joe Yates had talked of, food from another world.

Then something came along that was to change everything. It was the simplest food imaginable, yet so perfect, so comforting, soothing and fragrant. The dish contained only two ingredients. Potatoes, which were thinly sliced and baked in cream. There was the subtlest hint of garlic, barely present, as if it had floated in on a breeze. That pommes dauphinoise, or to give its correct title, pommes alla dauphinoise, was quite simply the most wonderful thing I had ever tasted in my life, more wonderful than Mum's flapjacks, Joan's lemon meringue, and a thousand miles away from anything I had made at college. Warm, soft and creamy, this wasn't food that could be a kiss or hug, like marshmallows or Irish stew, this was food that was pure sex.

The Bistro

'You mean you've never been to London?' said Andy, incredulous. You'd have thought I had just admitted never having heard of the Beatles. And with that we climbed aboard the college coach to Victoria and the dubious delights of a catering exhibition called Hotelympia.

Like most students forcibly attending such annual events we whizzed round the show's corporate stands quicker than you can say automatic-napkin-dispenser, then headed for somewhere, anywhere, less mind-numbing. We grabbed our two friends Sally and Clare, who had just been 'moved on' from the exhibition's hallowed Salon Culinaire for laughing at a sugar-icing replica of the Eiffel Tower (first prize), and fell into the nearest pub.

I had never been in a gay pub before. In fact, I'm not sure I even knew such a thing existed. Andy swore he only realised when he went to the men's room, though he chose not to elaborate on exactly what gave the game away. What-ever, he emerged shaken rather than stirred. Something I put down to his having been to public school. The four of us spent the afternoon getting quietly but paralytically drunk, then heading back to St Ermin's, our hotel in Victoria.

I had no intention of sleeping with Sally, nor she with me. It just sort of happened. Andy and Clare would occasionally toss a pillow at us and mutter something about having to get up later to go out for dinner. I told them we were just working up an appetite. Either way, I walked around with that I've-just-had-a-shag look on my face for the rest of the weekend. We took in the soft red plush carpets of Fortnum & Mason and the echoing marble of Harrods Food Hall. We tiptoed round Jackson's of Picca-dilly and waded through the streets of Chinatown with its rank and exotic odours and rails of glistening mahogany-coloured ducks. We drank cocktails in the 007 bar at the

Hilton, more in the modern splendour of the Inn on the Park, and then still more at a bar in Shepherd's Market that Andy had chosen specifically in the hope of showing us some upmarket hookers. 'I think we must be a bit early,' he said, clearly disappointed at the dearth of working girls. Clare and Sally went off to visit some friends of theirs who lived in Wimbledon. Andy and I went out to dinner and we all arranged to meet up again later.

Our meal was in a cosy, scrubbed pine bistro with low ceilings and pretty waiters who flirted with everyone, regardless of age or sex. I had yet to realise this was purely a matter of soliciting tips rather than an out-and-out mating call. A bistro where the flickering candles ensured an atmosphere just that bit too romantic for two guys to be comfortable dining together. Especially for one who played rugger at weekends. It didn't help that the waitresses clearly assumed we were a couple, even though we did rather play up to it. Or at least I did, partly to wind Andy up, partly because it felt strangely comfortable. The meal was absurdly rich – Campari sodas followed triangles of fried Camembert in breadcrumbs with a redcurrant and orange dip, then portions of saltimbocca the size of Jersey. We finished with profiteroles and hot chocolate sauce, pretty much the obligatory dessert that year. Andy had suggested a Chinese but I refused, making up a tale about being allergic to monosodium glutamate. It was one thing to have a shag in front of your more worldly best mate, another thing altogether to admit you had yet to master chopsticks.

Toast 3

I failed my exams, much to everyone's amusement. 'You'd have been all right if they hadn't included your accounts and economics results,' scoffed one of my lecturers who knew numbers had never been my thing.

I turned up in London one Tuesday morning with a backpack and just enough money for a couple of rounds of toast and a frothy coffee at a café on the Strand. I asked an old guy emptying rubbish bins in the dark, stinking loading bay of the Savoy if they had any jobs and he just pointed towards the flaking, subterranean corridors that wound their way under the hotel. He was still there, hosing down his vast garbage skip, when I emerged with a crisply starched white jacket over my arm, bearing the proud legend 'Savoy Grill'.

'They don't have anywhere for me to stay,' I shrugged. He shook his head and gave a weary little laugh, like he had seen it all a million times before. 'Best thing you can do is walk up to Piccadilly Circus and stand outside Swan & Edgar's,' he said. 'There will be someone who'll ask you if you want a bed for the night soon enough.'

'What, just like that?' I asked.

'Yes, son,' he smiled. 'You'll be fine, you'll be just fine.'